Welsh Colleges Scheme

Teacher Training Materials

For trainee teachers of Welsh
as a second language in the primary sector

Geraint Wyn Jones (Editor and Director)
Nia Royles (Language Criteria)
Lisa Jên Davies (Methodology Criteria)

GERAINT WYN JONES

Geraint Wyn Jones has been involved with second language teaching since 1960. In that year he was one of the founders of the Coleg Harlech Welsh Language summer school. During that period he also wrote the first Welsh language learning correspondence course for the NEC, Cambridge. Since then he has been instrumental in establishing a summer school at Bangor, and the National Eisteddfod 'Learner of the year' competition.

After moving to Bangor in 1970 he was involved in the training of teachers. During this period he published books and articles on second language learning as well as on literary topics. Before he retired in 2002 he was Director of Canolfan Bedwyr, at the University of Wales, Bangor.

LISA JANE DAVIES

Originally from Blaenau Ffestiniog, Lisa Jane Davies spent most of her working career in the old county of Clwyd teaching Welsh as a second language (SL) in the primary and secondary sectors before becoming the Welsh Language Organiser for the Authority. During this period she co-ordinated the work of the Athrawon Bro and the successful 'Further Professional Studies' courses for teachers who were learning Welsh.

After retiring from her role as Primary Link Officer for Denbighshire in 1997 she has been involved in numerous Welsh SL projects such as the translation of the popular 'Sbeic' series of 'Big Books' for KS2 pupils and the co-authoring of 'Ffeil-o-Fflic', a series providing a variety of reading materials for learners in KS2 and 3. She recently completed a factual book for older learners, entitled 'Cymeriadau' (Characters).

In 2001, she was appointed co-ordinator of the team writing ACCAC's 'Optional Assessment Material for Welsh Second Language in KS2'. She is the current University of Wales 'Welsh Colleges Scheme' External Examiner.

NIA ROYLES

Nia Royles started her teaching career as a Welsh SL teacher in Bargoed and has been involved with Second Language teaching ever since. She was a member of the panel that decided on the 'Cymraeg Byw' written forms of Welsh, and of the groundbreaking team that taught the first Welsh Ulpan in Cardiff. When she moved North she was appointed head of Welsh at Prestatyn High School before becoming Welsh Adviser for Clwyd at the time when the National Curriculum and assessing according to national criteria were being introduced to schools. She has wide experience in the field of examination and assessment.

First published in 2003 by:
Yr Ysgol Addysg, Prifysgol Cymru, Bangor,
Safle'r Normal, Bangor, Gwynedd LL57 2PX
© University of Wales, Bangor

Prepared for publication by @ebol
Layout and cover design: Ceri Jones
Cover photograph: Arvid Parry Jones
Printed by Cambrian Printers
ISBN 1 842200 13 5

Contents

Introduction

From the outset, the aim of the **Welsh Colleges Scheme** was to teach non Welsh-speaking trainee teachers enough Welsh to be able to present the language to the primary children of Wales. Initially, the Welsh Joint Education Committee's 'Graded Language Objectives' were used to assess their linguistic achievement. Over the years, however, it became increasingly evident that those objectives were not wholly appropriate for the task. For one thing, their aims were of necessity of a general nature. Trainee teachers needed specific targets. This, briefly, was why the Higher Education Funding Council for Wales funded a project to create new criteria in 1999-2000.

As the project got under way a joint decision was taken to change direction. It was felt that an adaptation of the National Curriculum second-language levels would be more appropriate. One advantage would be the fact that the levels are independent of any age. Another, the fact that teachers could concurrently acquaint themselves with pupil assessment. The team also decided to offer suggestions and examples of the kind of activities needed to achieve the levels. Examples of assessment at the various levels would also be given.

Eventually it was decided that National Curriculum Levels 1 and 2 would be combined for the adult audience. Another decision was that trainee teachers should be given a choice of paths. **The first path** would progress from Level 5 of the National Curriculum to *'Defnyddio'r Gymraeg'* (the adult equivalent of GCSE) of which levels A-C are adjudged to correspond to National Curriculum Levels 6-8. The advantages of taking this route would be:

(a) that the examination is specifically designed for the adult learner
(b) that the examination corresponds to an acknowledged qualification
(c) that the examination is sufficiently different to offer those already with a GCSE a worthwhile confidence-boosting experience

The **other corresponding path** would measure proficiency against National Curriculum Levels 6 and 7 and was intended to facilitate the Assembly's future intention that trainee teachers should have the same qualification in Welsh as is currently required in primary ICT (Level 7).

Participating institutions were also eager to assess methodology. After all, the *raison d'etre* of the B.Ed. degree is the training of teachers. When adapting the levels it was therefore decided to create methodological criteria. In this case, rather than define grades, it was decided to:

(i) define the pedagogic 'ideal' and then, using the Estyn five point scale,
(ii) measure the skills of trainee teachers against the 'ideal'.

This approach, it was felt, would familiarise future teachers with the very yardstick being used in their own appraisal.

As the definitions were based on language teaching essentials, the assessments could also be used for diagnosis. The exact strengths of trainee teachers could be recorded and aspects (linguistic or educational) needing further attention brought to the fore.

The Main Features of the Material

- The Welsh Colleges Scheme is divided into four parts:

    PART 1: LANGUAGE LEARNING CRITERIA

    PART 2: LANGUAGE TEACHING METHODOLOGY

    PART 3: APPENDIX

    PART 4: VIDEO TAPE OF ORAL AND READING WORK WITH EXPLANATORY NOTES

- The material is intended as a guide for trainee teachers and the content is available in both Welsh and English. Having read the English version it is hoped that trainee teachers will become increasingly familiar with the material in Welsh.

- Although the aim is to steep the trainee teachers in the National Curriculum, the exact wording of the document is not always retained. For example:

(i)   'expressing opinion' occurs much earlier in the present document, specifically to remind us that expressing 'like' (or 'dislike') can also be classed as 'expressing opinion'. Experimenting with language need not wait for 'official' approval.

(ii)   when a linguistic feature is discussed, it is taken for granted that it will then receive attention from that level onwards.

(iii)   in this documentation phrases like 'a wider range of words' (which the official document seeks to avoid) are used much more liberally to prevent trainee teachers from standing still.

Two further comments need to be made:

1.   Trainee teachers will be assessing their **pupils** according to **National Curriculum** levels.

2.   'Possible examples' are merely included for the sake of convenience. They should not be regarded as the benchmark of a language level. A relevant linguistic item can, generally speaking, be taught at any level.

The Material:

- enables the mentor or college tutor to photo-copy material

- is available as a constant resource during teaching practice

- is an useful checklist - for use by tutors and mentors during shared weeks (school and college)

- provides a video-tape to illustrate the kind of work that can be done at the different levels – accompanied by brief explanatory notes

- provides examples of written work at various levels.

It is hoped that the new order and its accompanying resources will assist colleges in ensuring continuity and progression in their Welsh language provision. The scheme should also prove useful to Local Education Authorities.

Acknowledgements

I am indebted to Nia Royles for adapting the language levels, to Lisa Jên Davies for her guidance on language teaching methodology and to Beryl Jones for an early translation. The project team would also like to acknowledge the following contributions:

- Non ap Emlyn and Geraint Wyn Jones for permission to include adaptations from *'Siarad Cymraeg yn y Dosbarth',* and *'Agweddau ar Ddysgu Iaith' (1993),* CAI, Llangefni.

- The WJEC (National Language Unit of Wales) for permission to reproduce excerpts from *'Datblygu Cymraeg Pob Dydd yn yr Ysgol Gynradd – Rhaglen Genedlaethol Hyfforddiant Mewn Swydd',* and to adapt an excerpt from *'Gwaith Pâr: Cardiau'r Plentyn'*

- The peripatetic Welsh language teachers (*Athrawon Bro*) of Conwy, Denbighshire, Flintshire and Wrexham for permission to use examples of their work

- The Publishers of *'Gemau Cyfathrebol Harrap'* (Jill Hadfield: adapted by Dafydd Hughes Pritchard for Clwyd County Council) for permission to use examples of their activities

- Non ap Emlyn and J. Philip Davies for permission to quote from *'Dulliau Dysgu'*

- Non ap Emlyn for permission to use an example from *'Siarad Cymraeg yn y Dosbarth',* The University of Wales, Bangor (1996)

The Steering Committee offered guidance throughout the project and, under the chairmanship of Professor Gareth Roberts, the University of Wales Education Subject Panel oversaw the implementation of the scheme by the participating institutions. Finally the project team would like to thank the Higher Education Council for Wales for funding the project.

Geraint Wyn Jones,
Canolfan Bedwyr, University of Wales, Bangor.   June 2003

Membership of the 'Welsh Colleges Scheme' Steering Committee

Geraint Wyn Jones: Chairman, (University of Wales, Bangor)
Nia Royles (Project team)
Lisa Jên Davies (Project team)
Steve Morris (University of Wales, Swansea)
Ann Tegwen Hughes (University of Wales, Bangor)
Kris Sobol (University of Wales College, Newport)
Brin Jones (University of Wales, Swansea)
Lynn Childs (Trinity College, Carmarthen)
Nia Richards (U.W. Institute, Cardiff)
Pam Evans-Hughes (NEWI, Wrexham)
Judith Lewis (U.W. Institute, Swansea)
Dilwyn Roberts-Young (University of Wales, Aberystwyth)
Richard Roberts (WJEC)
Iolo Dafydd (Estyn)

Part 1
LANGUAGE LEARNING CRITERIA

LEVELS 1 & 2

Focus Statement

The accreditation of trainee teachers with a LEVEL 1 & 2 certificate signifies that their language proficiency matches National Curriculum (second language) Levels 1 & 2 .

This means that the trainee teacher:

- is able to LISTEN and RESPOND appropriately in familiar situations

- can SPEAK audibly and clearly using a range of patterns

- can (as a result of oral experience) recognise familiar words and phrases in their written form

- is able to WRITE elementary phrases and sentences

Reference may also be made to **Cymraeg Pob Dydd,** WJEC.

Levels 1 & 2: Listening Assessment Criteria Level 2

Trainee teachers can show an understanding of short items spoken by a familiar voice by responding to them either non-verbally or in short oral phrases and listen to a range of stimuli including phrases, instructions, stories and verses. They can:

1. Understand greetings

2. Understand normal classroom directions

3. Respond non-verbally

4. Understand instructions and respond accordingly with simple actions e.g. music and movement, art and craft and everyday activities

5. Understand and respond non-verbally to verbs

6. Listen to familiar and unfamiliar voices e.g. to suitable excerpts from stories, songs and verses on tape and to suitable excerpts from television programmes

Possible Structures/Activities: Levels 1 & 2

1. *Bore da, Prynhawn da, Sut dach chi/ydych chi?*

2. **Class rituals:** at play-time, lunch-time, tidying up time, television time, end of school day. *Dere/Tyrd yma, Dewch yma. Eisteddwch, Gwrandwch, Edrychwch, etc.*

3. *Sefwch wrth y drws. Eisteddwch ar y gadair. Gwrandwch ar y stori. Edrychwch ar y llun.*
    Canwch gyda/ efo fi.
    Dim siarad. Dim rhedeg.
    Grŵp coch: sefwch, cerddwch, mas
    â chi/allan â chi, yn dawel/yn ddistaw.

4. *Yn ôl/ymlaen*
    i fyny/lan, i lawr
    yn araf, yn gyflym, yn ddistaw, yn uchel.
    Torrwch, rhowch, gludwch, tynnwch.
    Faint o'r gloch ydy hi?
    un, dau, tri o'r gloch, etc.

5. *Crïo/llefain, nofio, chwarae, rhedeg, mynd, canu, siarad, peintio, dawnsio, stopio, cario, etc.*

6. See: Level 2 Reading
    The *'Parablu'* series with **Tilsli** and **Madam Fflur**.
    The simplest tapes from the 3D series, etc.

Levels 1 & 2: Oracy Assessment Criteria
Level 2

Trainee teachers can seek, understand and convey simple information and respond to a wider range of stimuli. They can respond appropriately in simple, familiar situations using intelligible pronunciation and intonation, varying their vocabulary and patterns to a degree. They can:

1.   Greet and establish a relationship, greet friends

2.   Take part in activities, dialogues and role-play

3.   Converse with peers and other pupils

4.   Express feelings: like, dislike, need, etc

5.   Respond in short phrases

6.   Seek information: enquire and ask for things

7.   Convey simple information

8.   Convey personal and imagined experiences using suitable words, expressions and more than one sentence pattern

9.   Play a board game

★ Note
Sometimes linguistic items are 'prematurely' introduced to enable pupils to express their experiences. On this occasion **'Es i'** is introduced so that the children can refer to past experiences.

Possible Structures/Activities: Levels 1 & 2

1.   *Helô/Hylô*
Bore da, Prynhawn/Pnawn da
Sut wyt ti? Sut ydych chi?
Da iawn diolch. Bendigedig. Dw i'n/Rwy'n hapus
Gweddol. Go lew. Wedi blino. Ofnadwy.
Dw i'n dost/ sâl. Mae … yn dost/yn sâl
Beth sy'n bod?
Hwyl/Hwyl fawr. Da boch chi. Nos da

2.   [P   = Pupil]
P1:   *Pnawn da*
P2:   *Pnawn da*
P1:   *Pwy wyt ti?*
P2:   *Pry Bach Tew*
        Wyt ti'n hoffi Pry Bach Tew?
P1:   *Ydw*
P2:   *Pwy wyt ti?*
P3:   *Mili Malwen*
        Wyt ti'n hoffi Mili Malwen?
P2:   *Ydw*
P3:   *Hwyl*
P2:   *Hwyl*

3.   *Oes gen ti chwaer/frawd?*
Oes chwaer/brawd gyda('da)ti? Sawl un?
Mae gen i … Does gen i ddim … Mae chwaer gyda ('da) fi / Does dim chwaer 'da fi.
Beth ydy/yw dy oed di? Faint yw dy oed di?
Beth ydy/yw enw dy ysgol di?

4.   *Dwi'n hoffi/Rwy'n hoffi … Dw i ddim yn hoffi … Wyt ti'n hoffi? … Ydw/Nac ydw. Dw i/Rwy'n hapus. Dw i'n drist. Dw i ddim yn drist …*

5.   *Diolch, dim diolch. Ydw, Nac ydw. Oes, Nac oes. Os gwelwch yn dda. Dyma …; Yma. Ar y … Yn y …*

6.   *Ga i.. ? + classroom items – pensil, rwber, creon, papur … Ga i fynd i'r toiled ? Cei/Na chei. Cewch/Na chewch. Beth wyt ti eisiau? Wyt ti eisiau … ?*
Dw i/Rwy eisiau …

7.   *Gareth ydw i. Mae Tilsli/Wcw ar y silff.*
Teacher: *'Sut mae'r tywydd? Ydy hi'n … ?*
Pupil: *Mae'n braf , bwrw glaw, bwrw eira, oer, wyntog.*
Practise days of the week every day.

8.   *Rydw i'n chwarae pêl.* **Es i** ★ *i nofio ddydd Sadwrn. Mae Bili Broga'n drist.*

9.   *Pwy sy nesa? Fi, Fe/Fo.*
Learn to count 1 – 10.
All colours + adjectives
gwallt brown/llygaid glas
+ mawr, bach.
Shapes – *cylch, sgwâr, petryal, triongl.*

Levels 1 & 2: Reading Assessment Criteria
Level 2

Trainee teachers can recognise simple and familiar words and phrases (within their experience), and begin to show an interest in written material, by reading some simple passages. They show an understanding of what they have read by responding to the content either orally or non-verbally. They can:

1. Read (and listen to others reading) children's literature

2. Listen to a story being read and follow it in print – stories that are simple in language and characterisation

3. Read poetry and songs that are repetitive in pattern, rhythm and rhyme

4. Imitate the voice of a character whilst presenting or repeating an event in a story (simple role-play)

5. Read aloud their own work, and that of other authors

6. Read a variety of printed and computerised material

7. Read individual words and guess their meaning. Use dictionaries to search for a word or words

---

Other reading experiences
- Re-reading passages previously enjoyed
- Memorising passages.

- Choosing a wide variety of books to read and enjoy.

Possible Resources/Activities:
Levels 1 & 2

1/2 The 3D series e.g. **'Bili Broga'**, **'Helpwch fi'**, **'Mewn Hen Dŷ'** together with the listening tapes
The **'Paent Gwlyb'** series
'Anifeiliaid Difyr'
'Ble mae Dewi Deinosor?'
'Dau Gi Bach' – book and poster
'Troed yn taro' and listening tape
'Caneuon Parablu' – listening tape and video
'Sali Mali'; 'Aros funud' – Book and video tape
'Sali Sws', etc.

3. **Nursery rhymes** e.g. *'Mi welais Jac y Do'; 'Gwen a Mair ac Elin'.* Songs and nursery rhymes can also be modified for pupils e.g.

Original: *Awn am dro i frest, pen, coed …*
Adaptation: *Mynd am dro i frest, pen, coed …*

4. See Example 2 in **Oral** 1/2

5. For example **'Sali Mali'** or a simple dialogue such as Example 2 in **Oral** 1/2

6. **'Can gair cyntaf'**
'Y Geiriadur Lliwgar'
'Fy llyfr geiriau cyntaf'
'Geiriadur 1'
Charts, signs, strips, on-screen instructions, games, e.g. those accompanying the **'Magi Ann'** reading series.

7. Guess the meaning of *'ci mawr'* and *'ci bach'* using pictures. Use the **'Paentio Llun'** book where the character himself has to guess the meaning.

Levels 1 & 2: Writing Assessment Criteria
Level 2

Trainee teachers can communicate by writing words, phrases and a few sentences. Simple words are usually spelt correctly. They can:

1. Write phrases and short sentences in response to various stimuli

2. Write simple creative pieces

3. Write to communicate factual information

4. Write a short note, using phrases and some sentences, to a friend

5. Write short passages which express an opinion

6. Write for different audiences

7. Punctuate and spell commonly used words correctly.

8. Present their work clearly and neatly, using ICT whenever possible.

Possible Structures/Activities
Levels 1 & 2

1. **Television Programme**
   Hwre! Dw i'n hoffi Madam Fflur.

   Describe a **picture**
   Mae dau gi bach yn mynd i'r coed.

   Flash cards printed on the computer –
   Tedi yn y bath …

2. Write **a simple story** about a friend
   Mae Sam yn hoffi reidio beic. Mae o'n mynd i dŷ nain ar y beic.

3. **An event on the calendar** – as an e-mail:
   Dydd Mercher dw i'n mynd i'r Sŵ.

   An experience: entry in a diary
   Es i i Oakwood/Rhyl heddiw.

   Christmas shopping list – put on e-mail:
   Trên i Tomos, dol i Samantha, llyfr i Dad, sgarff i Mam.

   Present information about a friend
   Mae Dylan yn byw yn 18, Ffordd Rhuddlan, Caerdydd. Dw i'n hoffi chwarae pêl efo Dylan [fe/fo/hi] yn y parc.

4. **Party Invitation**
   Tyrd i'r parti. Dydd Mercher. Yn 17, Ffordd yr Eglwys, Sgeti.

   Note
   Dw i'n mynd i Oakwood gyda … ddydd …

5. **Express like/dislike**
   Rydw i'n / Rwy'n hoffi Samantha.
   Dw i /Dydw i ddim yn hoffi tomatos.
   Mae Darren yn neis.

6. **Write a birthday card to family members**
   Pen-blwydd hapus i Sam a Samantha

1. 'Speaking with intelligible intonation and pronunciation' means speaking correctly and clearly, using an increasing range of vocabulary and sentence patterns reasonably correctly.

2. The learners will extend their written work by adding a word or a phrase to the basic sentences.

3. They will also use dictionaries and personal vocabularies.

> **Additional Note**
> The structures/activities are obviously intended for classroom use. It is taken for granted that the material will be adapted (where necessary) for use with trainee teachers.

Focus Statement

The accreditation of trainee teachers with a LEVEL 3 certificate signifies that their language proficiency matches National Curriculum (second language) Level 3.

This means that the trainee teacher:

* is able to LISTEN and RESPOND appropriately to a series of brief items in familiar situations

* is able to use a wider range of vocabulary, phrases, sentences and questions ORALLY. The trainee teacher will volunteer some statements and convey simple information clearly

* has extended the ability to READ and understand a growing range of words in familiar contexts and has begun to develop as an independent reader

* is able to WRITE short, basic sentences using suitable vocabulary and patterns

* is following an integrated programme in which all the language skills – oracy, listening, reading and writing – are being developed

Reference may also be made to **Cymraeg Pob Dydd**, WJEC

Level 3: Listening Assessment Criteria

Trainee teachers show an understanding of a series of short items, spoken by a familiar voice, by responding non-verbally or orally. They can seek and clearly understand simple, personal and factual information ... This entails **listening** to a range of visual and audio-visual stimuli and to a variety of people. They can:

1. Listen carefully to, and show that they understand, a series of short items

2. Understand an increasing range of questions

3. Respond appropriately in varying situations

4. Understand an increasing range of directions

Possible Structures/Activities

Trainee teachers will consolidate Levels 1 & 2 by continuing to listen to and understand an increasing range of words, phrases, sentences and questions.

1. *Rhowch y cadeiriau dan y bwrdd / y ford ...*
   Sefwch y tu ôl i'r drws. Ydych chi'n barod?
   Pa liw wyt ti eisiau / isio? Melyn?
   Beth wyt ti'n baentio? Beth wyt ti'n baentio'n felyn? Haul? Ie?

2. *Pryd wyt ti'n codi? Beth ydy / yw enw dy chwaer di? Faint o'r gloch ydy hi? Un, dau, tri o'r gloch. Add hanner awr wedi, chwarter i, chwarter wedi etc. Pryd mae amser cinio? Faint ydy Kit Kat?*

3. For example: *Cadwch y paent. Dewch yma. Gwrandwch.*

4. *Dere / Tyrd yma, Dewch yma. Eisteddwch, Gwrandwch, Edrychwch, etc. Sefwch wrth y drws. Eisteddwch ar y gadair.*
   Gwrandwch ar y stori. Edrychwch ar y llun, etc. Canwch gyda / efo fi. Dim siarad. Dim rhedeg.

   i fyny, i lawr, ar y dde, ar y chwith, trowch i'r dde, trowch i'r chwith, yn ôl, ymlaen, yn ymyl, wrth ochr, etc.

   Grŵp coch: sefwch, cerddwch, mas â chi / allan â chi, yn dawel / yn ddistaw

   Playtime, lunchtime, tidying up time, television time, end of day rituals.

Level 3: Oracy Assessment Criteria

Trainee teachers can - seek and convey simple personal and factual information clearly, and make some statements voluntarily; speak with intelligible pronunciation and intonation using an increasing range of vocabulary and structures fairly correctly, for example, phrases, sentences and questions; add adjectives and verbs such as: *gweld, gwisgo, chwarae gyda/efo, prynu*, etc; introduce short forms and different persons of the verb as necessary – *Mi es i … Weles i … Fwytodd o/hi*, etc. and *'wedi'* with verbs. They will learn to use money, extend comprehension of prepositions, count 1-100, use days and months (e.g. birthdays of individual pupils or trainee teachers), express possession – *Mae gen i*, etc. *Pwy biau … ?* denote receipt – *'Cael'*, join pronouns and verbs – *edrych ar*, etc., use personal prepositions – *imi, iti*, etc., *Mae'n rhaid imi*, etc. They will respond appropriately in various situations. They can:

1. Seek (ask for) and understand simple, personal information

2. Seek and understand simple factual information

3. Convey simple, personal information

4. Ask permission

5. Express an opinion in simple terms

6. Volunteer comments

7. Engage in role play using short phrases (making use of television characters, characters in pictures/books, imitating the teacher or class friend)

8. Take part in a variety of dramatic activities and presentations, e.g. class assembly and/or class productions celebrating special days

9. Take part in group or class discussion on a variety of subjects

10. Improve their grasp of idiomatic Welsh

Possible Structures/Activities

1. *Beth ydy dy oed di? Beth ydy oed Mam? etc. Mae gen i/gyda fi … does gen i ddim … Oes gen ti/gyda ti ('da ti) chwaer/frawd? Sawl brawd sydd gen/'da ti? Sut wyt/ ydych chi? Da iawn, diolch.*

2. *Beth ydy enw dy ysgol di? Oedd hi'n stormus neithiwr? Oedd/Nac oedd. Oes gen ti anifail anwes? Beth ydy'i enw fo/hi? Wyt ti eisiau … ?*

3. *Dw i/Rwy i wedi blino. Dw i wedi mynd i'r gwely'n hwyr/am 11 o'r gloch. Rwan/nawr, dwi'n dost/sâl. Mae'n rhaid i fi fynd at y doctor.*

   Roedd y Celtiaid yn byw mewn tŷ crwn.

   Roedd hi'n stormus ac yn wyntog neithiwr.

4. *Ga i* + more classroom items. Connect *Ga i* with verbs: *Ga i/Gawn ni weld?* etc. *Cei/Na chei. Cewch/Na chewch.*

5. For example, about school /films/ television/ hobbies, etc. *Dw i'n hoffi/casáu blas hufen iâ siocled. Dw i'n mwynhau CD Catatonia. Dw i ddim yn hoffi coch. Dw i ddim yn hoffi ffilm cowbois.*

6. *Wyt ti wedi gweld y ffilm 'Chicago'? Dw i eisiau chwarae gêm fwrdd, plîs, Miss.*

7. P1: *Pwy wyt ti?*
   Dracula: *Drac ydw i.*
   P1: *Beth sy'n bod? Rwyt ti'n edrych yn ofnadwy.*
   Drac: *Dw i eisiau diod.*
   P2: *Pop, lemonêd, coca-cola?*
   Drac: *Na! GWAED!*

8. Present a prepared script:
   P1: *Joseff ydw i. Rydw i'n mynd i Jerwsalem.*
   P2: *Mair ydw i. Rydw i'n mynd i Jerwsalem hefyd …*

9. Discuss television programmes, sports, food, hobbies, computer games, school, etc

10. Collect idioms such as – *heb siw na miw, andros o oer, yn wên o glust i glust*, etc. from such series as 3D.

Level 3: Reading Assessment Criteria

Trainee teachers can understand and respond simply to texts containing an increasing range of words and phrases, to short passages in familiar contexts and read simple texts in an increasingly appropriate manner. They also begin to read independently and show an interest in the material. They can:

1. Read and listen to others reading a range of imaginative material – both prose and poetry written specifically for learners, e.g. material which presents a challenge in length and vocabulary, which repeats structures, vocabulary and rhyme – and some authentic material intended for the native speaker

2. Listen to a story being read and follow it in print, e.g. using reading stations/overhead projector

3. Choose books independently from a range of texts, and read voluntarily because the text appeals

4. Convey the content of materials read with appropriate characterisation e.g. create a dialogue of part of a story and perform it in pairs

5. Recall materials read and re-read them. Retell the content of passages that were enjoyed

6. Use some technical terms to discuss the text, e.g. *awdur*/author, *cynllun*/plot, *disgrifiad(au)*/description(s)

7. Search for information and present it orally and in writing

8. Read their own work and other printed texts aloud, accurately, with meaning and appropriate expression, and with increasing confidence

9. Use a wide range of reference material and other documents

Possible Resources/Activities

1. **Prose**: e.g. *'Taid a'r sosej'*, *'Bwli'*, *'Busnesa'*, *'Lladron Sam'*.

    Poetry: e.g. *'Ymolchi mewn cwstard'*, *'Lola'r Lindys Barus'*.

    First language material: e.g. *'Y Pry Bach Tew'*, **Cyfres y Bont**, *etc.*

2. Tapes of books or teacher's readings, etc.

3. For example: *'Sbeic yn y parti'*, *'Un noson dywyll, dywyll'*.

4. **Dialogue** such as the one found in Example 2, **Llafar** 1 & 2 based on *'Beic Ben'*, *'Edi Esgus'*, etc.

5. *Roeddwn i'n hoffi stori* **'Sbeic yn y parti'** *achos mae Sbeic yn ddoniol.*

6. T: *Wyt ti'n hoffi'r llyfr? Pam?*
    P: *Mae'r plot yn dda. Rydw i'n hoffi … /Dw i'n hoffi …*
    T: *Y lluniau?*
    P: *Mae (pointing) yn dda ond dydw i ddim yn hoffi … (pointing).*
    T: *Pam?*
    P: *Achos …*
    T: *Oes ofn yn y stori?*
    P: *Wel mae … yn gas.*
    T: *Beth am yr awdur (author)?*

7. Use aids such as: *'Y Geiriadur Lliwgar'*; *'Y Ditectif Geiriau'*; *'Mrs Morgan y Milfeddyg'*, etc.

8. Regular opportunities should be offered.

9. For example, ICT materials, catalogues, magazines, information books, reference books.

Level 3 : Writing Assessment Criteria

Trainee teachers can write short basic sentences, using suitable vocabulary and patterns and fairly correct syntax. They spell simple words correctly and show some awareness of basic punctuation e.g. using capital letters and full stops with some consistency. They can:

1. Write in response to a variety of stimuli

2. Write brief basic phrases and sentences

3. Use suitable vocabulary and patterns in a variety of *genres*

4. Adhere to the characteristics of *genres* when writing for different purposes

5. Write for various audiences, both real and imaginary

6. Write a variety of documentary passages

7. Create passages on a range of subjects which present a view and express an opinion

8. Express opinions and give reasons in support

9. Develop the ability to - link sentences and phrases intelligibly, use a variety of structures and use paragraphs effectively.

Equipment for the experiment

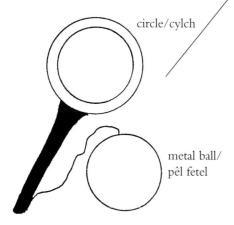

circle/cylch

metal ball/
pêl fetel

Possible Structures/Activities

1. **Describe a picture or pictures**
   Fill 'speech bubbles' in 2/3 cartoon pictures.
   Television programme
   Mae Madam Fflur yn siarad yn 'posh'. Mae hi eisiau …

2. **Event / Story**
   Roedd tân mewn siop. Roedd injan dân yno.
   Doedd neb wedi brifo/cael dolur, etc.
   Experience
   Roeddwn i yno (+ the event/experience).

3. **Menu** for a class member's birthday party.
   Shopping list compiled by Madonna at Christmas.

4. **Post card to Mum** – *Annwyl Mam, Rydw i'n mwynhau Alton Towers. Rydw i wedi bod ar y …*
   Wela i di …
   Letter to Miss Evans: *Annwyl Miss Evans, Diolch yn fawr. Rydw i'n/wedi hoffi dysgu Cymraeg gyda/efo chi. Hwyl. Rydw i'n mynd i Wolverhampton ddydd …*
   Cofion Janine

5. **E-mail message**
   7.30pm *Wedi mynd i'r sinema. Dewch i'r Olympia.*
   Letter giving information, written on computer:
   Annwyl Sharon, Roedd Alton Towers yn wych. Mae dosbarth Miss … yn dda. Ond roedd … yn ddrwg ar y bws. Mae Janine wedi mynd i Wolverhampton.

6. **Record** the steps of a **simple experiment** (see below): *Rydych chi'n rhoi'r bêl yn y cylch. Mae'r bêl yn mynd drwy'r cylch. Rydych chi'n poethi'r bêl. Dydy'r bêl ddim yn mynd drwy'r cylch. Mae hi wedi 'chwyddo'.*

7/8. After watching a television programme, **create a chart** showing likes and dislikes

Enw'r rhaglen ……………………………………		
Wedi hoffi	*Wedi casáu*	*Achos*
……………	……………	……………

9. Example of adding simple information and linking sentences:
   Yn Alton Towers mae … , … a …
   Rydw i wedi mynd ar y … a …

Focus Statement

The accreditation of trainee teachers with a LEVEL 4 certificate signifies that their language proficiency matches National Curriculum (second language) Level 4.

This means that the trainee teacher:

- is able to LISTEN, UNDERSTAND and RESPOND orally within familiar situations to a variety of spoken contributions

- can use a wider range of vocabulary, phrases, sentence patterns and questions orally. The trainee teacher will be more confident and able to begin to develop his/her own ideas.

- has extended the ability to READ and understand the general sense of a text. The trainee teacher is developing as an independent reader and is able to read familiar extracts clearly

- is able to WRITE conjoined sentences using suitable vocabulary and phrases having begun to develop ideas logically

- is following an integrated programme in which all the language skills – oracy, listening, reading and writing – are being developed

Reference may also be made to **Cymraeg Pob Dydd,** WJEC.

Level 4: Listening Assessment Criteria

Trainee teachers have become accustomed to different voices and display an understanding of the general sense of materials presented in familiar contexts. They respond both non-verbally and in short phrases. They can:

1. View and **listen** to a range of (i) visual (ii) audio-visual stimuli and (iii) to a variety of people

2. Understand an increasing range of words, phrases, sentences and questions

3. Understand the 'vocabulary' of a wider range of fields and themes

4. Understand a series of directions

5. Show an improved grasp of idiomatic constructions

6. Show an awareness of some dialectic variations

7. Display an increasing awareness of colourful phrases and sayings

Possible Structures/Activities

1. Listen to different teachers talking.
   (Listen to tutor/class friends/college friends).
   Watch dramatic productions in school, theatre in education, etc.
   View (and become acquainted with characters from) television programmes and videos such as **'Bobol Bach', 'Gwyliau George',** etc.

2. Understand the language used at such times as: break-time, lunch-time, games period, end of the day:
   Rydw i'n mwynhau …
   Gawsoch chi/Gest ti?
   Beth ydy dy gyfeiriad/rif ffôn di?
   Beth wyt ti'n gael i frecwast?
   Wyt ti wedi bwyta malwod yn Ffrainc?
   Ble roedd … yn gweithio?
   Ydyn nhw'n cerdded i'r gwaith?
   Ble est ti ar dy wyliau?
   Sut est ti? Pam est ti? etc.

3. Understand: money *(adio, tynnu a rhoi newid)*; size *(rhy fach, rhy fawr)*; all the months of the year; more detailed time *(deg munud i, ugain munud wedi … etc.)*; discussions about such subjects as – hobbies, holidays, interesting events, games *(enilloch chi/enillaist ti'r gêm? Pwy enillodd? Ti sgoriodd? Bydda i'n gweld y gêm heno).*

4. *Ewch at y goleuadau, trowch i'r dde/chwith, gofynnwch i …, ewch ar hyd, cerddwch ymlaen, edrychwch am …*

5. *Gan/cael – mae gen i annwyd. Mae ganddo fo/fe … Mae ganddi hi … Does dim … ganddo fe/fo. Mae'n gas gen i /well gen i/ rhaid i fi. Rydw i'n cael beic, etc.*

6. *Rwan/nawr; taid/tadcu; dere/tyrd; mas/allan; e/o; fe/fo; brwnt/budr.*

7. For example: *Malu'n racs jibidêrs. Mynd fel malwen. Cysgu'n andros o hwyr. Wrth fy modd …*

Level 4 : Oracy Assessment Criteria

Trainee teachers can present information and talk about some experiences as they begin to develop their own ideas. When speaking, their pronunciation and intonation is intelligible and they use an increasing range of phrases and sentence patterns, with some accuracy ... They respond appropriately in various situations and speak clearly, confidently and for the most part correctly. They can:

1.   Present information

2.   Speak with peers and pupils and begin to form second language relationships

3.   Take part in presentations and dramatic activities of all kinds

4.   Play various character roles, enact situations in response to stimuli and begin to develop their own ideas

5.   Express opinions in simple terms

Possible Structures/Activities

1.   **Present facts / feelings** in their conversations:
Mae Madonna yn dod o America. 'Dyn ni'n mwynhau gwrando ar Madonna. Mae e/hi'n hoffi blas hufen iâ Haagen Daz. Rwy'n casáu gweld ... ar y teledu. Roeddwn i'n/Roen i'n casáu gwynt/ ogla ... Roedd o'n mynd dros ben llestri yn ...

2.   As in Level 3 **increasing in confidence**
P1: *Sut wyt ti/ydych chi y bore' ma?*
P2: *Ddim yn ddrwg, diolch.*
P1: *Wyt ti ddim wedi blino'n lân?*
P2: *Nac ydw.*
P1: *Mae hi'n braf heddiw.*
P2: *Ydy. Roedd hi'n ofnadwy ddoe.*
P1: *Oedd. Maen nhw'n dweud bydd hi'n braf yfory hefyd.*
P2: *Grêt.*
P1: *Wela i ti /chi.*
P2: *Hwyl rwan.*
Add family members in question and answer sessions: *Yncl, Anti, cefnder, cyfnither. Pryd mae pen-blwydd Yncl John?*

3.   See: Example 7, Level 3, Oracy.

4.   **Role-play** – impromptu activities
Making a purchase (using: *punt – dwy bunt, tair punt; ceiniog – dwy geiniog, tair ceiniog, hanner can ceiniog*). Telephone conversation, doctor questioning a patient, policeman questioning a thief. A situation from a video/book ... etc.

5.   P1: *Rydw i'n casáu codi yn y bore achos rydw i'n hoffi cysgu ...*
P2: *Tan? ...*
P1: *Deg o'r gloch.*

6. Contribute in group or class discussion on a variety of subjects	6. **Discuss** an **event** as affected by e.g. … *y tywydd. Roedd + tywydd adeg trychineb* (disaster) *y llong olew yn Sir Benfro. Oedd hi'n? Oedd/Nac oedd.* Discuss pop music; football teams; computer games; school trips; friends, dramatic presentations watched, characters from television programmes and books similar to those listed in the Appendix.
7. Use an increasing range of words, phrases, sentences and questions	7. More: • Verbs + prepositions – according to context *Es i i'r gwely am … (Ddaru mi fynd, etc). Aethon ni i Alton Towers gyda … yn ymyl, dros y ffordd i …* • Adjectives: *tal/byr, trwm/ysgafn, etc.* • Adverbs: *yn araf, yn gyflym, yn ofnus … etc.*
8. Use more comparisons	8. *Gwyn fel yr eira, araf fel malwoden, cyflym fel y gwynt, tew fel mochyn, etc.*
9. Recite or sing Welsh songs and poems containing sentence patterns. Some will have been modified	9. *Roedd Ffrits o wlad Awstria … Ar ben Waun Tredegar … Dyn bach o Fangor wedi dod i'r dre … Mae gen i het dri chornel …* (See: **Caneuon i Ddysgwyr**).
10. Show an improvement in the use of idiomatic Welsh	10. *Mae'n rhaid i mi/ti,* etc. *Cael* = to allow: *Ydw i'n cael mynd?* (Am I allowed to go?)

Level 4 : Reading Assessment Criteria

Trainee teachers show that they understand the general sense of paragraphs or short conversations in familiar contexts by recognising key words, phrases and facts. They are able to respond to the materials read referring to significant details. They develop as independent readers and, when reading aloud, read clearly with a degree of expression. They can:

1. Read and listen to others reading a range and variety of fictional material which is more challenging in length and vocabulary

2. Use context to find meaning

3. Use a wide range of information books and other documents including ICT materials

4. Choose books independently from a number of texts and read them voluntarily because the content appeals

5. Recall what has been read having re-read extracts which were enjoyed

6. Read publicly in a correct and confident manner with meaning and appropriate expression

7. Use more technical terms to discuss a text

Possible Resources/Activities

1. Read poetry and stories which, although still containing repetition, are more challenging e.g. The **'Nici a Cris'** series by Mari Tudor.

   Continue to listen to stories being read - using reading stations/overhead projector – following them in print.

2. Read a line or two of a text and ask the pupils/trainee teachers to guess who said the words and what they meant.

   Ask questions about a passage e.g. *Pam doedd Sbeic ddim yn hoffi'r ysgol?*

3. Search for information (about people, events, pop songs, recipes, etc.) from catalogues, magazines, books, pamphlets, the Web, etc. and present it orally and in writing.

4. (See examples of suitable books for specific ages in the Appendix).

5. Retell e.g. part of a story, an interesting recipe, an amusing anecdote, to the class.

   Convey the content of material read using appropriate characterisation – imitating the character's voice.

   Create a dialogue from part of a story and act it out in pairs.

   Trainee teacher's own work and /or other printed resources.

7. Terms such as *awdur*/author, *cynllun*/plan, *disgrifiad*/ description, *deialog*/dialogue, *dylunio*/design, *clawr*/ cover, *broliant*/blurb. e.g. after reading from the **'Sbeic ac eraill'** series (WJEC, for Levels 2, 3 and 4).

   Rydw i'n hoffi'r stori. Mae ... yn ddoniol achos ... Mae'r disgrifiad yn dda achos ...

   (In the above example there would be an opportunity for the tutor to present the term *disgrifiad*/description and read the relevant example).

Level 4 : Writing Assessment Criteria

Trainee teachers can write linked sentences showing some grasp of organisation and sequence. They use suitable vocabulary and phrases, vary patterns and produce basic sentences which are fairly accurate. They spell most structure words correctly and, where necessary, use punctuation – capital letters, question marks, apostrophes and full stops – accurately on the whole. They can:

1. Write, in a series of phrases or basic short sentences, in response to a variety of stimuli

2. Write a variety of documentary and factual pieces using a series of brief basic sentences

3. Write original pieces based on experience

4. Write for different audiences including the teacher, family and friends, and imaginary audiences

5. Exploit the features of a *genre* when writing for different purposes

6. Express an opinion and present a view on a range of subjects – supporting the viewpoint with reasons

7. Plan, draft and improve work and discuss it with others

Possible Structures/Activities

1. Give a **factual description of a picture** e.g. Botticelli's *Spring*
   Mae afalau ar y coed ac mae blodau ar y llawr. Yn y llun mae chwe merch hardd. Mae tair yn dawnsio ac mae Ciwpid yno. Edrychwch ar y dyn cryf! Ydy e'n hoffi'r ferch? Mae hi mewn cariad!

2. **Record the 'story' of a television programme**
   Mae Mrs Murphy wedi colli modrwy. Mae'r fodrwy wedi mynd i lawr y sinc. Mae John Ogwen wedi ffeindio'r fodrwy. Ond mae e wedi cadw'r fodrwy. Yn y dafarn …

3. *Roedden ni'n chwarae yn erbyn ysgol Drefach ddydd Sadwrn. Mi wnes i sgorio dwy gôl ffantastig. Ond ddaru nhw sgorio chwech …*

4. **Letter – conveying information**
   Annwyl S4C,
   Rydw i / Rwy'n mwynhau gwylio'r Murphys. Mae'r plot yn dda ac mae'r actio'n dda hefyd. Dydd Sul, rwy'n gwylio omnibws Pobol y Cwm. Rydw i/Rwy'n hoffi Karen ac yn casáu Teg.
   Diolch. (See also 7 below)

5. **E-mail – an invitation to a party:** *Mae parti yn tŷ ni ddydd Sadwrn. Wyt ti'n gallu dod? Nigel.*
   Shopping list: *creision, siocled, coca-cola, cardiau Pokemon, CD, etc.*
   Poster: *Dewch i chwarae rygbi i'r pentref.*
   Postcard: (based on the first pages of **'Yr Hen Dŷ'**)
   Annwyl Mair,
   Sut wyt ti ? Sut mae'r criw? Doeddwn i ddim eisiau symud. Ond heno, mae pawb yn mynd allan/mas i gael pizza. Rydw i'n mynd gyda Rhian, Eira, Steve a Rhys. Bydda i'n ysgrifennu eto. Plîs dw i eisiau llythyr gen ti a'r criw.

6. After watching a television programme, create a simple questionnaire and conduct a simple survey by using it with four members of the class. Then make a chart showing their likes and dislikes.

7. Suggestion regarding redrafting a letter (see 4 above):
   Step 1 – divide it into two paragraphs, the first discussing the 'Murphys' and the second talking about **Pobol y Cwm**.
   Step 2 – add details to the first paragraph e.g. Mae'r plot yn dda ac yn syml.
   Step 3 – add more **Pobol y Cwm** actors' names to paragraph 2 and state … *Rydw i'n hoffi … Dydw i ddim yn hoffi …*

Trainee Teachers:

- Become more confident in linking prepositions with verbs: *edrych ar, gwrando ar, cerdded at, mynd at,* etc.

- Use a dictionary and personal vocabulary lists to improve the quality of language – to record the meaning of a word (in its context) and to note the relevant prepositions (when appropriate).

- Pay attention to spelling and punctuation, to writing words in their standard written form and to neat and clear presentation.

- Note idioms from books, and record and use them.

- Develop some ideas of their own. There is also more variety in the language used.

- Plan, draft and improve their work and discuss it with others.

- Make constant use of ICT.

- Continue to develop the ability to use a variety of constructions.

Focus Statement

The accreditation of trainee teachers with a LEVEL 5 certificate signifies that their language proficiency matches National Curriculum (second language) Level 5.

This means that the trainee teacher:

- is able to LISTEN and RESPOND to longer items in familiar situations

- is able to display growing oral confidence and make statements which show an awareness of sequence and progression. He/she can initiate conversation and substantiate statements with a few simple reasons. He/she can speak clearly and intelligibly using a wider range of phrases, sentence structures and verb forms

- can READ, and understand the general sense of a range of materials. He/she can read independently and express simple opinions on materials read. He/she can read aloud clearly and with expression

- can WRITE, develop ideas and show a grasp of organisation and sequence. He/she can express opinions simply using a suitable variety of syntax

- is following an integrated programme in which all the language skills – oracy, listening, reading and writing – are being developed

Reference may also be made to **Cymraeg Pob Dydd,** WJEC.

Level 5 : Listening Assessment Criteria

Trainee teachers can understand longer items in familiar situations and respond to them. The KS2 study programme, intended for those who teach Year 6, remains the basis of study. The additional requirement in listening and understanding is the ability to understand *longer items*. They can:

1. Listen to a range of (i) visual (ii) audio-visual stimuli and (iii) to a variety of people

2. Respond appropriately to a variety of situations

3. Follow a change in tense within familiar situations – from the Present to the Past or Future

4. Understand an increasing range of vocabulary, phrases, sentences and questions

5. Understand a wider range of colourful expressions

6. Understand and respond to directions/ commands – *wch* and the second person singular

7. Understand more variations in dialect

8. Show an improvement in their understanding of idiomatic Welsh

Possible Structures/Activities

1. Widen and deepen the experiences noted in Level 4 using such learning resources as *IAW! Clwb Clebran, Cwmni 292* and current suitable children's programmes.

   Learn to follow the antics of television programme characters.

2. Understand more vocabulary in conversations. Begin to understand subject-specific language e.g. health, sport; language registers – i.e. the style relevant to a particular context e.g. talking to a friend, to a headmaster/headmistress.

3. Listen to experiences of 'yesterday' and 'today' and hopes for 'tomorrow' in a variety of fields – e.g. holidays, football …

4. *Fuost/Fuest ti? Glywaist ti? Pa bryd? Pwy biau? Wnest ti ddeall? Beth gest ti gan … ? Pwy wnaeth … ? etc.*

5. According to theme and context:
Fear	*yn ddigon i godi gwallt y mhen*
Rain	*yn pigo bwrw, yn arllwys/tywallt y glaw*
Snow	*eira mân, eira mawr*
Movement	*fel cath i gythraul*
Mood	*ar bigau'r drain, wedi rhoi'r ffidil yn y to, mewn hwyliau da, ar ben ei ddigon.*

6. *Dos; Cer; Sbïa; Yli/Ylwch; Sgwl ma/Edrycha.*

7. *Moyn/eisiau; da/gwartheg; gwynto/ogleuo; brwnt/budr; losin/da da/mincieg.*

8. Phrases such as: *malu awyr; siop siafins;* Idiomatic constructions such as: *gwrando ar, gwrando arno fe/fo, arnyn nhw. Mae gan/gyda fi, gyda ni, chi, nhw. Does dim … ganddon ni, ganddoch chi, ganddyn nhw. Does/doedd dim rhaid … Mae'n gas gen i/ well gen i … Roedd rhaid i fi. Bydd gen i/ arna i annwyd yfory. Bydd gen i/gyda fi arian ddydd Gwener, etc.*

Level 5: Oracy Assessment Criteria

Trainee teachers can initiate conversations, show greater confidence, and some awareness of sequence and progression. They can give a few simple reasons to support their ideas. They speak intelligibly and fairly fluently using a variety of phrases, sentence patterns and verb forms and display a good measure of accuracy. They can:

1. Talk to peers and pupils and develop second language relationships

    Respond appropriately in various situations

2. Develop some of their own ideas using more linguistic variety.

    Use an increasing range of vocabulary, phrases, sentences and questions.

    Use a variety of verbal forms

3. Speak correctly, clearly and confidently with a good degree of accuracy.

    Respond to others' statements and sometimes change the direction of a conversation, etc.

4. Take part in all kinds of presentations and dramatic activities

Possible Structures/Activities

[The additional requirement in L5 is the ability to **develop** some ideas]

1. Develop oral styles according to context – e.g. a conversation with a friend, a headmaster/headmistress, etc.

2. Convey feelings in a conversation: *Rydyn ni'n mwynhau gwrando ar … Rwy i'n casáu gweld … ar y teledu. Roeddwn/Roen i'n casáu gwynt/ogla … Mae e/o'n mynd dros ben llestri. Mi fydd Dad/Mam yn flin/grac!*

    As in Level 4 but showing more confidence and some awareness of sequence and progression:

    Roedd y gêm gyfrifiadur yn grêt. Ond doedd Mam ddim yn hoffi'r sŵn.

    Varying the tenses and persons of verbs: *Aethon ni; Ges i; Wela i; Byddan nhw; (Ddaru chi weld/Naethoch chi weld? Welsoch chi?) Fyddwch chi? Fasech chi? Pryd basech chi?*

    Use a range of prepositions: *Yn ymyl y llyn, fe welson ni Rhodri Morgan yn cerdded rhwng y plismyn tuag at y car.*

3. P1: *Beth wyt ti'n meddwl o dîm rygbi Cymru?*
    P2: *Dim lot!*
    P1: *Tîm Cymru ydy'r gorau!*
    P2: *Mae'n gas gen i/'da fi rygbi. Mae'n well gen i bêl-droed.*
    P1: *Wyt ti awydd/eisiau chips?*
    P2: *OK.*

    Tell an interesting anecdote based on a newspaper/magazine article/Web picture, etc.

4. Present a prepared script (Here, again, the progress from the previous level is indicated by the confidence with which the script is presented)

5. Play differing character roles. Create scenes of conflict in response to stimuli. Begin to develop their own ideas

6. Contribute to a group/class discussion on various subjects

7. Express an opinion in simple terms, offering some evidence/reasons

8. Present information

9. Make use of more comparisons

10. Recite or sing Welsh songs and verses which contain suitable patterns or idioms, etc.

5. Here, progress can be seen in the characters' response to each other, the confidence evident in conversations in familiar situations and the ability to initiate and steer a conversation e.g.

P1: *Rydw i'n casáu codi yn y bore achos rydw i'n hoffi cysgu …*
P2 : *Tan?*
P1: *10 o'r gloch …*
P2: *10 o'r gloch?*
P1: *Ie. Pam lai?*

More challenging situations can be set such as: coming home late and arguing with Mum/Dad.

6. Discuss an event that is within the experience of the group using several verb forms (as required): *Oedd hi'n? Oedd/Nac oedd/Bydd/ Ydy? Fuost ti/Welodd o … ?*

7. *Roeddwn i'n cael aros yn y gwely heddiw achos roedd Mam …*

8. Present interesting information about people, events, pop songs, recipes, fashions, computer games, etc.

9. Employ a wider range of adjectives/comparisons:

yn denau fel brws, yn dal fel postyn lamp, yn ddu fel bol buwch, yn dew fel mochyn, etc.

10. *'Sgen ti sws imi?'* – Caryl Parry Jones
'Chwarae'n troi'n chwerw' - Caryl Parry Jones

'Pam fod eira'n wyn?' – Dafydd Iwan

'Mae bys Meri Ann wedi brifo'

Level 5 : Reading Assessment Criteria

Trainee teachers can respond to a range of suitable material showing understanding of the main ideas, events and characters, select relevant information and express opinions in simple terms. They can read independently and read aloud clearly and with expression.

[The emphasis in L5 is on the material being 'challenging both in length and vocabulary']. They can:

1. Read aloud accurately, confidently, with meaning and appropriate expression

2. Use context to extract meaning, keeping the wider context in mind as a checking device

3. Select books independently from a range of texts and read, voluntarily, out of interest in the content

4. Seek information from a wide range of reference books, documents, ICT materials, etc. and present it orally and in writing

5. Recall read material after re-reading extracts which have given delight

6. Select different kinds of books and enjoy them. Retell the extracts which were enjoyed

7. Discuss materials read using more appropriate terms

8. Continue to use a dictionary to look for words and their meanings

Possible Resources/Activities

1. Select part of a story and read to class. Picture(s) and diagrams will be shown to engage the interest of the 'audience'. (See methodology section.)

   Read a wider and increasingly challenging selection of prose and poetry e.g. from **Urdd magazine**s and **Cwmni 292** publications, etc. (See Appendix.)

   Listen to others reading a range of imaginative material either live or in a 'listening station'. The teacher may use an overhead projector to display the print.

2. Read a line of text. Invite the students to guess who said the words, why they were said and what they mean.

3. See Appendix for a list of books suitable for the age range being taught.

4. Look in catalogues, magazines, reference books, recipes, information sheets, pamphlets, booklets, Web material …

5. Retell these either to contemporaries in the group or class, or produce an oral report for radio or television.

6. Convey the content of material read using appropriate characterisation. Create a dialogue based on part of the story and act it out.

   Read the work of other trainee teachers e.g. their anecdotes. Read further printed material.

7. Introduce such terms as *awdur, cymeriad, cefndir, awyrgylch, datblygiad plot, disgrifiad(au), diweddglo, stori …*

   Rwyf/Rydw i'n mwynhau llyfrau Bob Eynon. Mae'n **awdur** *da. Mae e/o'n apelio at blant ifanc yn y llyfr 'Yr Hen Dŷ'. Mae* **plot** *gydag ysbrydion yn apelio. Ond mae plot da i fyfyrwyr ac oedolion yn y llyfr 'Y Llythyr'. Yn y* **stori** *mae Bob Eynon yn* **disgrifio** *teulu – mam a chwaer sy'n byw yng Nghymru a hanes Tom a Steve yn Bosnia. Roedd un o'r milwyr o Gymru wedi marw yn Bosnia.*

8. The trainee teacher underlines about four or five 'new' words in a paragraph and asks the class to find their meaning with the help of a dictionary and/or context. The meanings can be agreed as a group activity.

Level 5 : Writing Assessment Criteria

Trainee teachers can write linked sentences, and develop their ideas showing a grasp of organisation and sequence. They can select vocabulary and phrases suited to the purpose, show some variation in their sentence patterns, and produce structures and sentences which are fairly correct. They can express opinions simply, spell most of the words within their experience correctly, and punctuate appropriately using inverted commas where necessary.

[Progress at Level 5 is seen in the ability to select suitable vocabulary and phrases and introduce more variety in sentence structures. It is also displayed in the ability to write in an organised manner 'showing a grasp of order and sequence', that is in an improved ability to use paragraphs effectively]. They can:

1. Write in various factual and fictional genres (stories, simple poems, word-portraits, etc.) in response to a variety of stimuli

2. Write for a variety of audiences including teacher, family and friends and imaginary audiences.

    Learn a little about *genres* and use the features of these *genres* when writing for different purposes

3. Write various factual pieces

Possible Stuctures/Activities

1. **Describe an experience** – factual
    Going to watch a football game; playing in a football game; recent holidays; going to a disco; a dream.
    Retell the story of a television programme – factual
    Roedd Mrs Murphy wedi colli modrwy, modrwy briodas, i lawr y sinc. Doedd hi ddim eisiau colli'r fodrwy. Felly galwodd hi'r plymwr. John Ogwen oedd y plymwr ac fe ffeindiodd o'r fodrwy. Ond roedd o'n twyllo Mrs Murphy ac yn cadw'r fodrwy. Yn y dafarn y noson honno …
    Describe an experience – imaginative
    Ideal holidays; a meeting with a man from space; a meeting with a celebrity …
    Short dialogue (phone conversation)

Megan:	*Helo Gina.*
Gina:	*Wel helo, Megan. Sut wyt ti?*
Megan:	*Da iawn. Dw i'n dod i Gaerdydd ddydd Sadwrn.*
Gina:	*Grêt. Wela'i ti o flaen Marks am 11 o'r gloch. Beth am fynd i Da Mario's am ginio?*
Megan:	*Bydd y cinio'n costio bom. Ond dim ots. Mae fy mhenblwydd i ddydd Sul. Bydda i'n talu. Celebration bach!*
Gina:	*Waw! Diolch Megan. Ond na! Bydda i'n talu. Fy anrheg pen-blwydd i i ti.*

2. **Postcard** – Based on a reading experience.
    Party menu – in the form of an e-mail.
    Invitation to a dance.
    Poster – devised on a computer, inviting people to join a Yoga class.
    News bulletins
    Biographies of contemporary heroes
    Cartoon strips
    Simple books for younger children

3. **Letter** – presenting information:
    Annwyl S4C,
    Bob Dydd Sul rwy'n gwylio omnibws Pobol y Cwm. Rydw i'n hoffi Karen a giamocs Mark. Rydw i/Rwy'n dysgu lot o Gymraeg achos y subtitles.
    Diolch.
    Simple notes; Diaries; simple experiments, etc.

4. Write pieces which express opinion and a point of view on a range of subjects

5. Plan, draft and improve work, in discussion with others

Language development

- Make regular use of ICT. This will facilitate the redrafting and improvement of work.

4. **Questionnaire:** *Ydych chi'n hoffi'r rhaglenni plant ar y teledu? Beth ydych chi'n hoffi? Beth dydych chi ddim yn hoffi?*

   Write a report expressing the views of the class.

5. Improve the work by extending the report after listening to others in the class. Improve the level of expression and accuracy of syntax.

Note: Occasionally, redrafting can lead to 'new' work e.g. 'compare the above reports in a group and then produce a composite one.'

Focus Statement

The accreditation of trainee teachers with a LEVEL 6 certificate signifies that their language proficiency matches National Curriculum (second language) Level 6.

This means that the trainee teacher:

- has increased his/her oral skills, as a listener, observer and speaker

- is able to SPEAK fluently with appropriate pronunciation and intonation and with increasing confidence within a range of formal and informal situations

- has been taught to READ a variety of texts of increasing difficulty both for his/her enjoyment and to seek information

- has been encouraged to develop and express informed personal opinions both ORALLY and in WRITING based on his/her reading

- has been taught to produce material in a number of WRITTEN *genres* using different styles, a range of accurate sentence patterns and textual structures appropriate to the task

- is developing his/her abilities within a programme in which oral, listening, reading and writing skills are deliberately integrated. The learning opportunities bring together the requirements of the Range, Skills and Language Development sections of the National Curriculum.

Reference may also be made to **Cymraeg Pob Dydd**, WJEC.

Level 6 : Listening Assessment Criteria

Trainee teachers can show that they understand the spoken language, used in a range of familiar situations, by selecting specific details. In discussion, they can listen to contributions made by others and suitably respond to them. They can:

1. Understand everyday conversation

2. Understand dialect and different accents

3. Understand extracts from plays and/or other visual stimuli

4. Listen and respond appropriately and courteously to what is said

Possible Structures/Activities

1. Listen to and watch an expanding range of radio and television programmes – greetings, record requests, phone conversations, news items, suitable clips from television programmes/series/videos intended for learners.

2. Watch/listen to extracts from such programmes as *'Hel Straeon', 'Rownd a Rownd', 'Wedi 7', 'Pobol y Cwm'*, etc. Complete watching/listening tasks (see *'Llunyddiaeth'* G. W. Jones, 1995) based on these excerpts. Note the language used by characters from different backgrounds – *nawr/rwan; fo/fe; bechod/trueni; brwnt/budur.*

3. Watch suitable excerpts from soap operas and note which characters speak in a similar way. (See 2 above).

4. Understand the kind of constructions used in discussions e.g.

Conversation 1
Rydw i'n cytuno gyda/efo Megan. Mae cath(od) yn boen. Ond rydw i'n hoffi ci/cŵn. Mae dau gi gen i ac maen nhw'n grêt.

Conversation 2
Roedd Tracy yn dweud fod ... yn ... Ond dydw i ddim yn cytuno achos ...

Conversation 3
Rydw i'n cytuno gyda/efo ...
Mae David Beckham yn grêt/dda. Ond dydw i ddim yn cytuno bod ... yn well na fo/fe. Mae Zidane/Anelka yn ...

Level 6 : Oracy Assessment Criteria

When expressing an opinion the trainee teachers can agree or disagree and give reasons to support that view. They can speak freely using an increasing range of phrases and sentence patterns and vary the time and person of the verb correctly as a rule. They can:

1. Express opinions in discussion

2. Use various forms of agreement/disagreement

3. Give reasons and evidence to support and defend a viewpoint (or to persuade)

4. Use the standard spoken language accurately

5. Use a range of phrases, questions and sentence patterns accurately

6. Vary the time and person of the verb

7. Contribute and respond effectively

8. Convey personal experiences

9. Seek, receive and discuss information from different sources

Possible Structures/Activities

[One measure of progress between L5 and L6 is : Level 5 – speaks fairly freely; Level 6 – speaks freely]

1. Use such constructions as:
    Yn fy marn i mae … achos …
    Rydw i'n meddwl/credu bod … yn …
    Dydw i ddim yn cytuno gyda/efo … achos …

2. *Yn hollol; wrth gwrs; Ie wir; Ie Ie; Do Do;*
    Oes Oes, etc. Dim peryg/ Dim siawns; Nage wir;
    Na Na; Naddo wir; Nac oes wir, etc.
    Rydw i'n meddwl fod John yn iawn.
    Dydw i ddim yn meddwl fod John yn iawn achos …

3. P1: *Beth am barti ar ddiwedd y tymor?*
    P2: *Grêt, mewn gwesty?*
    P1: *Na yn fy nhŷ i. Mae digon o le.*
    P2: *Ond beth am y llanast/yr annibendod?*
    P1: *Paid â phoeni. Bydd John Bouncer yn dod.*
    P2: *O wel! Beth am y bwyd a'r diod?*
    P3: *A'r* entertainments.
    P1: *Does dim eisiau* entertainments.
    P2: *Wel oes wir!* etc.

5. For example phrases which contain comparison of adjectives – *Mae ei wallt o mor ddu â'r frân. Mae o'n dew fel mochyn. Mae o'n dwp fel bat, etc.*

6. E.g. : *Fe/Mi â i gyda/efo fo at y doctor. Fe/mi fyddwn i/faswn i'n …* more *'fy', 'dy'* etc. *rhaid/dylwn. Ces i fy ngeni/cafodd … ei eni/ei geni; arna i/amdana i/wrtho fe/fo,* etc. The negative with *mo/ddim o.*

7. (i) Individually e.g. get the children to use flash cards and the group to recognise them
    (ii) Groups of three to question each other
    Ble buest ti /buoch chi/ am wyliau yr haf diwethaf?
    Fuest ti / Fuoch chi yn … ?
    Ble byddi di / fyddwch chi'n mynd eleni?
    (iii) Report back to group/class

8. Discuss the weekend/hobbies/experiences, etc.

9. Discuss the advantages and disadvantages of physical exercise after gathering information from tapes, books, computers, current English and Welsh magazines, etc.

Level 6: Reading Assessment Criteria

Trainee teachers can show an understanding of suitable material, (including some authentic texts concerned with topics which are within their experience), by selecting the main points. They can obtain information on specific subjects from more than one printed source and use it appropriately. They can express opinion on materials read, and offer reasons to support a point of view. They can read extended texts independently and read aloud with increasing expression and confidence. They can:

1. Read a range of authentic fictional materials and those written specifically for learners

2. Read (and use) a range of non-literary texts (in a variety of forms) including formal and ICT material

3. Learn to scan texts to obtain a gist of the content

4. Find information, make notes and present the information clearly

5. Recognise different *genres,* understand the characteristics of various kinds of texts and note the manner in which orthographical devices, sounds and words can be used for effect

6. Develop as independent readers and maintain a personal reading programme

7. Interpret the content of material read by presenting it with appropriate characterisation

8. Read aloud their own work and other printed resources confidently, fluently and with meaning to engage an audience

9. Discuss a text and express an opinion on texts read

10. Recollect material read, re-read it and retell the extracts which gave pleasure

    Learn excerpts by heart

Possible Resources/Activities

1. Familiarise themselves with such series as *Cyfres Bibliobus, Cyfres y Rhwydi (Lefel 3), Cyfres IAW!, Cyfres y Canllaw, Cyfres Powics* and some of Bob Eynon's novels.

2. Select suitable materials e.g. information on forms, posters, information sheets, orders, short tracts from newspaper articles, etc.

3. Understand the main gist of a passage without necessarily knowing every word. Search quickly for specific details in leaflets, letters and forms.

4. Build a collection of printed material from *Sbeis / Cyfres 292 / Ifanc / Prentis /* local papers, etc. on the same subject – to find facts about historical characters, celebrities from the world of sport, etc. in order to present the information orally or in written form.

5. Discuss the differences in form between e.g. novels, letters, information leaflets, advertisements, etc. referring to sentence length, the use of large print, headlines, repetition, etc.

6. Present both factual and imaginative material – stories, novels, learners' magazines, etc. Foresee the conclusion after reading the beginning of a cartoon-strip or serial story in a learners' magazine.

7. Respond to a suitable poem or part of a novel through role-play.

8. Read a personal experience, hymn, poem, anecdote or suitable story in a school assembly.

9. (i)   Write a letter explaining why a certain book should/should not be read.
    (ii) Discuss analytically, recognising their forms, diaries, letters, paragraphs, cartoon-strips and techniques such as use of dialogue.
    (iii) Use such terms as *awdur, plot, disgrifiad, cwestiynau, brawddegau,* etc.

10. Learn traditional or modern verses or pop songs. Retell favourite parts of stories or novels read.

Level 6 : Writing Assessment Criteria

Trainee teachers can use language purposefully to give detailed accounts of experiences and familiar events, to record factual information and to give reasons to support their opinions. They use punctuation and paragraphing to produce clear, organised writing. They possess a fairly good grasp of syntax and any work produced will possess a 'Welsh flavour'. They can:

1. Write in a variety of contexts, for a range of purposes, using a range of suitable forms

2. Express personal and imaginary feelings

3. Present information and produce varied factual accounts

4. Express opinion in response to a range of printed, visual and computerised stimuli

5. (i) Extend and correct their language using various resources
    (ii) Make extensive use of ICT

6. Use appropriate vocabulary and terminology when discussing features of their work and that of others

Possible Structures/Activities

1. Write a: **story** appropriate to a certain age group; **report** for a magazine on a particular interest; **postcard** to a friend (informal); **letter** to a superior (formal).

2. Keep a holiday **diary**. Write a **dialogue** recording a row between friends.

3. Create a **list of tips** for Y6 pupils about to advance to Y7. Create an **information leaflet** to persuade pupils to use a certain shop. **Record**: the steps taken when 'marbling' in an art lesson, the stages of an experiment (e.g. growing a bean on damp cotton wool) in a science lesson, steps taken when following a recipe in a cookery lesson, historical information about a certain district.

4. **Fill in a form** which has a certain amount of room for extended writing. Write a letter on a contentious matter, etc.

5. (i)   Appropriately use dictionaries, vocabularies, personal notes, spell-checkers and grammar-checkers on the computer. Extend vocabulary and verb forms and develop their knowledge of grammar.
    (ii) Use spell-checkers, and by redrafting on a computer, produce posters, leaflets, newspaper articles, etc in appropriate format.
    (iii) Use the full range of punctuation.
    (iv) Pay careful attention to mutations and spelling and write the majority of words acccurately.
    (v)   Create effect by – repetition, varying sentence length, use of adjectives, recording conversation, etc.
    (vi) Develop their writing skills by concentrating on: paragraphing, organisation of ideas, expression.

6. For example: *ailadrodd*/repetition, *disgrifiadau*/descriptions, *brawddegau*/sentences, *paragraffau*/paragraphs, *penawdau*/headings, *print mawr*/large print, etc.

Focus Statement

The accreditation of trainee teachers with a LEVEL 7 certificate signifies that their language proficiency matches National Curriculum (second language) Level 7.

This means that the trainee teacher:

- has become more effective and confident in ORAL situations

- exhibits an increasing ability to initiate and make substantial contributions to discussions

- can tailor his/her language to specific purposes, contexts and audiences

- can READ increasingly challenging texts

- can pay attention to detail, in order to reformulate, discuss and combine information

- can WRITE purposefully and at length, building on previous work

- can improve and polish his/her writing in a wide range of *genres*, paying appropriate attention to accuracy, purpose and audience

- is developing within a programme in which oral, listening, reading and writing skills are fully integrated

- is provided with opportunities to combine the requirements of the Language Range, Skills and Development sections of the National Curriculum

- is provided with opportunities to use Welsh in social, professional and imaginative contexts

Reference may also be made to **Cymraeg Pob Dydd**, WJEC.

Level 7 : Listening Assessment Criteria

Trainee teachers show an understanding of and can respond to a range of spoken language which includes simple and complex sentences in a variety of contexts. In a discussion they can pay close attention to what is said ... They can:

1. Watch and listen carefully to a variety of visual and audio-visual stimuli paying attention to the language used and to intonation and mannerism

2. Recognise the main dialectic variations and regional accents and recognise some elements borrowed from English

3. Listen and respond appropriately and courteously to what they hear paying close attention to what is said

Possible Structures/Activities

[One measure of progress between L6 and L7 is:

L6 – listen carefully; respond with a question

L7 – pay close attention; question in order to acquire ideas]

1. Use clips from television programmes paying attention to the *informal* language of the garage, pub, dialogue between friends and acquaintances, and the *formal* language of the court, interview, committee, doctor and patient, headmaster and pupil, etc. Make a list of the variations in the language, intonation and mannerisms of each character. Decide on the most fitting words (from a list) to describe them:

Intonation: *yn dawel, yn bwyllog, yn bwysleisiol, yn chwareus, yn sarcastig, yn wyllt, etc.*

Mannerisms: *ysgwyd pen, codi bawd, crychu talcen, gwneud ceg gam, camu'n ôl, etc.*

Tone: *cyfarch fel ffrind, fel estron, etc.*

Listen to a phone message and relay it to others.

2. Watch a suitable extract from a soap opera or learners' video and (i) list the linguistic features of the different characters – *mas/allan, lan/i fyny, gwynt/ogla*, etc. and (ii) borrowed words e.g. OK. Try to give a general imitation of the speech of one or two characters.

3. Listen attentively and use appropriate mannerisms to reflect interest in the contributions of others. Follow this by elaborating on the points made, and questioning in order to promote discussion, etc.

Elaborating on Conversation 1 Level 6

P1: *Ond rhaid cadw cŵn mas/allan. Maen nhw'n gwynto/ogleuo.*

P2: *O na! Mae dau gi yn byw gyda/efo ni a dydyn nhw ddim yn gwynto/ogleuo. Dw i'n rhoi bath iddyn nhw bob wythnos.*

P1: *Tasai cŵn yn byw gyda/efo ni, basai Mam yn mynd yn wallgo. Mae'n casáu cael anifail yn y tŷ.*

Elaborating on Conversation 3 Level 6

P1: *Ffrainc ydy'r tîm gorau yn y byd rwan /nawr.*

P2: *O na! Mae tîm Man U yn well. Mae ... yn chwarae yn y tîm, beth bynnag.*

P1: *Ond chwaraeodd tîm Lloegr ddim yn dda yn Cwpan y Byd. A roedd pobl gorau Man U, Lerpwl a ... yn tîm Lloegr.*

Level 7: Oracy Assessment Criteria

In a discussion the trainee teachers can pay close attention to what is said, developing their conversation purposefully. They express opinions, occasionally using evidence. They speak freely and with some accuracy in a variety of situations and contexts and generally demonstrate a good grasp of the spoken language's natural syntax. They can:

1. Express opinion in discussions

2. Offer a variety of reasons and evidence to persuade or to support and defend a point of view

3. Use accurate, standard spoken language with confidence

4. Discuss a range of subjects dealing with varying points of view

5. Take part in dramatic presentations of all kinds

6. Contribute and respond effectively

7. Produce extended contributions when conveying personal and imaginary experiences

8. Present information, sometimes based on research, producing more extended contributions where appropriate

Possible Structures/Activities

[One measure of progress between L6 and L7 is:
Level 6 – speak freely ... varying the time and person of the verb accurately for the most part;
L7 – speak freely ... and generally demonstrate a good grasp of the spoken language's natural syntax]

1. Agree and disagree. Repeat key points. Refer to evidence from a number of sources.

2. and 3. – **School Rules**

P1: *Dw i'n casáu rheolau ysgol.*

P2: *Dw i'n cytuno ond mae'n rhaid i ni gael rheolau.*

P3: *Dw i'n cytuno efo/gyda'r rheol yma – mynd yn brydlon i wers.*

P2: *Ie. Rhaid gwneud y gwaith, rhaid gwneud y gwaith cartref a wedyn, rydych chi'n gallu pasio arholiadau.*

P1: *A beth am y rheol nesaf? 'Ni ddylech ddod â radio etc. i'r ysgol'. Ydych chi'n cytuno?*

P2: *Mae Mr. Jones wedi confiscato fy ffôn symudol i.* (laughing) *Roedd hi wedi canu yn y wers Saesneg!*

P3 : *Dw i'n cytuno. Ond dydw i ddim yn cytuno â thynnu cotiau a sgarffiau yn y gaeaf. A rydw i'n meddwl bod ni'n gallu gwisgo colur – tamaid bach – a bod bechgyn yn gallu torri gwallt fel maen nhw eisiau.*

The conversation goes on to discuss individual rules giving evidence for and against these and others. Perhaps one pupil will try to persuade the others to change one rule and speak about it in the School Forum.

4. Discuss the importance of eating well with a health visitor, or the arguments for and against having a McDonalds in town.

5.   (i) Role-play e.g. Visiting a Police Station to report a theft/*Mynd i Swyddfa'r Heddlu i adrodd am ladrad*

  (ii) Students' original work

  (iii) Published material

6.   (i) Individually e.g. Discuss a newspaper headline or a striking photograph/*Trafod pennawd mewn papur newydd neu lun trawiadol*

  (ii) Group discussion e.g. Discuss unemployment statistics/*Trafod ystadegau diweithdra*

  (iii) Report back to group/class.

7. Give a detailed and organised talk about a visit to a particular place using a map or a diagram as illustrations.

8. Discuss such ideas as cruelty to animals using details from articles, television programmes, etc.

Level 7: Reading Assessment Criteria

Trainee teachers can read and understand a selection of appropriate material (including some authentic material) by selecting and interpreting the main points. They can express opinions and refer to plot, character and key features in a text to support a viewpoint. They can retrieve and collate information from a range of sources and present extracts to others meaningfully and with confidence. They can:

1. Read a wide range of imaginative, authentic and learner-orientated materials

2. Read and use a wide range of non-literary texts including public and official formal material and ICT material

3. Scan to obtain the gist of material read

4. Obtain specific information from parts of a text and present it clearly and in appropriate form

5. Recognise different *genres* and understand the features of various texts in print and other media. Note the manner in which orthography, sound and words can be used for effect

6. Develop as independent readers and maintain a personal reading programme

7. Read aloud challenging extracts, from their own work and other printed resources, confidently, meaningfully, fluently and with appropriate expression, to engage an audience

8. Interpret sensitively what is read through appropriate presentation and characterisation

9. Recall what was read, re-read it and repeat the extracts which gave pleasure in addition to memorising some sections

10. Use a range of relevant terms when discussing various texts

Possible Resources/Activities

1. Continue with the more advanced novels of Bob Eynon, **Cyfres y Dolffin**, novels by Philip Davies, Ivor Owen, etc.
   Begin short, first language novels e.g. **'Eira Mawr'** by Islwyn Ffowc Elis.

2. Choose suitable materials e.g. information on forms, authentic leaflets, letters, faxes, e-mail messages, memos,etc.

3. Understand the main gist of an extract without insisting that the meaning of every word is known. Search quickly for specific details or information in letters, leaflets, memos, etc.

4. Read (i) part of a story gathering information in order to write a character description for the police; (ii) a number of factual texts such as advertisements, information leaflets, tickets, to create a week-end activity timetable.

5. Express an opinion on a range of subjects:
   • referring to aspects of content, form and style
   • making comparisons • noting similarities and differences between e.g. a cartoon strip and an unillustrated story with regard to content, form, length, use of dialogue and pictures, characters, etc.

6. Present factual and imaginative material in a range of forms – stories, novels, learners' magazines, etc.

7. (i) Read their own work to the class
   (ii) Take the part of various characters when undertaking class readings.

8. Demonstrate a knowledge of characters by dramatising part of a text and presenting it in written form and/or orally.

9. Learn traditional and contemporary verses or pop songs. Retell a favourite part of a story or novel.

10. Use such technical terms as: *ansoddeiriau, disgrifiadau, plot, awdur, ffurf, berfau.*

Level 7 : Writing Assessment Criteria

Trainee teachers can use language purposefully to describe familiar experiences and events in detail, to record factual information and to support their opinions with reasons. They can use punctuation and paragraphing to produce pieces of clear and organised writing. They have a fairly good grasp of syntax and any work produced will have an authentic 'Welsh' feel to it. They can:

1. Write in response to a wide variety of social, professional and imaginative stimuli using a range of suitable forms

2. Express personal and imaginary experiences

3. Present information using a range of factual/discursive writing

4. Express opinion in response to a range of printed, visual and computerised stimuli

5. Extend and correct their linguistic creations

6. Use appropriate vocabulary and terminology when discussing features of their own work and the work of others

Possible Structures/Activities

1. Write: a **story** suitable for a certain age; a **magazine report** on some topic of interest; a **review** of a television programme for a regional paper; a **message** to a friend discussing week-end arrangements (informal); a **letter** to thank a guest speaker (formal).

2. Write: a **letter** to a friend discussing important personal events; a **note** in a diary after meeting an 'idol'.

3. Produce: an **information leaflet** to advertise the local area; a **work-experience report** for a tutor, a **detailed description** of a Leisure Centre – to attract more customers. **Fill a form** (which has room for extended writing) describing a witnessed road accident.

4. Write: a **letter** to the press on a contentious subject; a letter to a magazine e.g. *Golwg;* a letter to the regional paper opposing the closure of the local hospital, using sub-titles, quotations, etc.

5. (i) Make appropriate use of dictionaries, vocabularies, personal notes, grammar and spell-checkers on computers, etc.
   (ii) Make extensive use of ICT e.g. spell-checkers, and opportunities for redrafting to produce posters, leaflets, newspaper articles in appropriate format, and/or set out an **agenda**
   or an **official report** in an appropriate manner.
   (iii) Use the full range of punctuation.
   (iv) Give careful attention to mutations and spelling and write the majority of words used accurately.
   (v) Use a wide range of linguistic techniques to create effects e.g. repetition, variation in sentence length, emphatic sentences, striking comparisons/contrasts, whilst extending vocabulary and verb forms.
   (vi) Develop their writing by paying attention to paragraphing, organisation and expression, and to deepening their knowledge of language in order to promote accuracy.

6. For example: *ailadrodd*/repetition, *disgrifiad(au)*/description(s), *berfau*/verbs,

ORAL

The **trainee teacher** will converse with **the tutor.**

1. He/She will:
    greet, give personal details, talk about the weather, and express liking.

    ★   The answers will be short and reflect comprehension. The trainee teachers will ask some questions. Various patterns will be used.

    e.g.   *Rydw i'n … (hoffi/ byw …)*
    (Enw) ydw i.
    Mae (discussing weather)
    with simple, familiar vocabulary

2. He/She will present personal information (2-3 short responses).

    e.g.   *Dw i'n byw yn … Rhif y ffôn ydy …*
    Enw Mam / y gŵr/ y plentyn ydy …
    Es i i ysgol …

READING

3. The **trainee teacher** will select a book at Level 1 or 2 and read a story aloud.

WRITING

4. The tutor will be presented with **four** pieces of written work **completed in class** e.g.
    (i)   a picture caption e.g.   *'Bangor yn y nos'*
    (ii)   a shopping list for a party e.g.   *gwin, bara Naan, cwrw, creision,*
                                                   teisen/cacen pen-blwydd
    (iii) a passage of 3-4 lines e.g.   *Rwy'n/Rydw i'n hoffi/Dw i ddim yn hoffi*
    (iv)   a story or information about a friend

ORAL

1. The **trainee teacher** will converse with the **tutor**, asking and answering questions and, discussing **personal details.**

2. The conversation will continue, progressing to **expressing an opinion on one or two subjects.**

   Subjects already broached by class members in Question 1 will be selected
   e.g. films/hobbies/games, etc.

   It is expected that opinions will be expressed using: *Roedd e/o'n dda. Rwy/Rydw i'n casáu/hoffi*

   The tutor **or a class member** can ask up to two questions.

3. The **trainee teacher** will **present personal or imagined information** about **Saturday morning** and about any **two** of the following:

getting up time	coffee time
time to dress	lunch time

   The trainee teacher will be required to **tell the time** once or twice either voluntarily or in response to one or two questions.

READING

4. The **trainee teacher** will select a book at Level 3 and orally (individually):
   (i) answer questions about the book
   (ii) act in role-play **with a partner** creating 4/6 responses and imitating the character's voice
   (iii) respond to the question – *Pam ydych chi'n darllen y llyfr ...* (title)? – using
   achos ... and discussing plot *(mae'n dda) ... lluniau*/pictures, *cymeriadau*/people

WRITING

5. The tutor will be presented with **four** short pieces of written work **completed in class**
   (as in Levels 1 and 2), e.g.
   (i) a description of an illustration
   (ii) a postcard to a friend asking for a Welsh book/discussing holidays
   (iii) a letter to Grandma about a holiday/a friend /a new game
   (iv) a chart expressing an opinion about 4 television programmes

ORAL

1. A **group of three** trainee teachers will converse together on the subjects listed below adding comments and widening the discussion as the situation requires:

    the weather, what food and clothes are preferred by teachers and/or pop groups

    ★   It is expected that the conversation will be intelligible, will contain some development of ideas, and a variety of patterns which will include:

    Mae/Roedd gen i, gyda fi. Mae'n gas gen i/well gen i/well gyda fi. Mae/roedd rhaid, etc. Rwy/Rydw i wedi gwisgo/bwyta, etc. as well as *bwytes i, gwisges i, ddaru mi/ wnes i ...*

The conversation will last for a few minutes.

READING

2. The **trainee teachers** will select a Level 3 or 4 book (which has been read by the group) and continue to work on it within the group.

Member 1:	will outline the story.
Member 2:	will cite interesting details expressing pleasure and opinion.
Members 1 and 3:	will respond to questions asked by the other two and, if necessary, to the tutor/examiner's questions.
Member 3:	will re-read aloud pieces relevant to the discussion.
The group:	will discuss using such words as *awdur, plot, lluniau, pobl (cymeriadau)* as they express an opinion about the book and possibly about others.

WRITING

3. The tutor will be presented with **four** pieces of written work **completed in class** e.g.

    (i)   an account of a past event or experience
    (ii)   a detailed advertisement for selling a house (as in the Saturday edition of the Western Mail), or a poster advertising an event e.e. *Twmpath Dawns*
    (iii)   a piece expressing an opinion on 4 television programmes/football games
    (iv)   an informative piece on a subject chosen by the trainee teacher

4. (i)   The trainee teacher will **read one of the above out aloud.**
    (ii)   He/She will **explain why he/she has chosen the piece** referring to the pleasure and problems experienced during its writing.

ORAL

1. A **group of three** trainee teachers will discuss familiar subjects among themselves adding comments and widening the discussion as the situation requires.

    ★   It is expected that the conversation will be intelligible, display confidence, contain some development of ideas and a variety of patterns which will include:

    Mae/Roedd gen i, gyda fi. Mae'n gas gen i/well gen i, well gyda fi. Mae'n rhaid, etc. Rwy/rydw i wedi gwisgo/bwyta as well as *bwytes i, gwisges i, ddaru mi/wnes i fwyta.* Trainee teachers will also be expected to be able to vary the persons of the verb/and personal prepositions *'gan'* and *'i'* i.e. *gwell ganddyn nhw/gyda nhw/rhaid iddyn nhw, etc.*

    The conversation will **last for a few minutes.**

READING

2. The **trainee teachers** will select a Level 4/5 book (which has been read by the group) and continue to work on it within the group.

Member 1:	will select a part of the story and relate it to the group.
Member 2:	will cite interesting details expressing pleasure and opinion.
Members 1 and 3:	will respond to questions asked by the other two and, if necessary, to the tutor/examiner's questions .
Member 3:	will re-read aloud pieces relevant to the discussion.
The group:	will discuss using such words as *awdur, plot, lluniau, pobl (cymeriadau)* as they express an opinion about the book and possibly about others.

WRITING

3. The tutor will be presented with **five** or more pieces of written work **completed in class** e.g.
    (i)   an account of a past event or experience
    (ii)   an original story
    (iii)   an opinion on a subject chosen by the trainee teacher
    (iv)   an informative letter to a friend on a subject chosen by the trainee teacher
    (v)   a short task – note, poster, menu, etc. using ICT

4. (i)   The trainee teacher will read one of the above out aloud.
    (ii)   He/She will **explain why he/she has chosen the piece** referring to the pleasure and problems experienced during its writing. Any re-drafting that has taken place will also be mentioned.

PATH 1:

1. Grades A-C of the 'Use of Welsh' examination are considered to correspond to Levels 6, 7 and 8 of the National Curriculum. The examination itself 'corresponds to the Welsh Second Language for Adults, GCSE'.

2. The following advantages pertain to following this syllabus:
   (a)   it offers a path towards an examination the value of which is generally recognised;
   (b)   it is an adult examination;
   (c)   there is sufficient difference between it and the ordinary GCSE to offer something different to the diffident candidate who has already obtained a Welsh (Second Language) GCSE;
   (d)   it will facilitate the provision of progressive INSET by Local Authorities.

PATH 2:

3. The other option is to follow the syllabus outlined in 'Possible Examples'. The assessment will then be made according to Levels 6 and 7 of The National Curriculum (Second Language)

4. Examples of:
   • Listening Comprehension Tests
   • Communication Tasks
   • Reading and Comprehension Tests
   • Written Tests

   that convey the nature of the assessments and the desired standard can be obtained from **WJEC, 245 Western Avenue, Cardiff, CF5 2YX**.

Part 2
LANGUAGE TEACHING METHODOLOGY: THE ESSENCE OF GOOD PRACTICE

		SECTION A: THE FOUNDATIONS OF GOOD TEACHING
	1.	Revision
	2.	Presenting language
	3.	Setting up an activity
	4.	Drilling
	5.	Classroom organisation
	6.	Motivating pupils to enquire/ask questions
	7.	Reporting back and receiving feedback
	8.	Concluding an activity/lesson
		SECTION B: ADDITIONAL SKILLS
	9.	Vocabulary selection
	10.	Correcting mistakes
	11.	Transferring language across contexts
	12.	Teacher questioning
	13.	Extending conversations
		SECTION C: WAYS OF ENRICHING LANGUAGE
	14.	Everyday Welsh
	15.	Using information and communication technology
	16.	Cross-curricular language teaching
	17.	Using video resources
	18.	Presenting a story
		SECTION D: READING AND WRITING
	19.	Reading
	20.	Writing
		SECTION E: OTHER RESOURCES AND TECHNIQUES
	21.	Role-play
	22.	Board/Class games
	23.	Flash cards
	24.	Pictures/illustrations
	25.	Displaying work
	26.	Using an Interactive White Board
		SECTION F: ASSESSMENT AND APPRAISAL
	27.	Self-appraisal
	28.	Tutor and mentor appraisals
	29.	Assessing pupils

Section A
The Foundations of Good Teaching

1. REVISION

WHY?
- to keep previous work at hand and fresh in the mind

WHEN?
- at the beginning of each lesson
- when necessary (or when a **natural** opportunity arises)

THINGS TO CONSIDER
Does the trainee teacher:
- use natural conversation to revise vocabulary, syntax, previous lessons, etc. - e.g. by referring to present/past television programmes, hobbies, etc?
- avoid revising the work in exactly the way that it was presented?
- revise by using familiar vocabulary and syntax within a 'new' activity?
- encourage the pupils to draw on resources already possessed, i.e. to cultivate the skill of language transfer?

  (See: Transferring Language across contexts Page 57).

2. PRESENTING LANGUAGE

WHY?
- to provide the language lesson with context and content
- to make the oral work (conversation/role-play) easier and more meaningful
- to prepare pupils thoroughly for communicative activities
- to establish a supportive ethos – that promotes language confidence and enjoyment

WHEN?
- in every language lesson

THINGS TO CONSIDER
Does the trainee teacher:
- explain clearly, briefly and purposefully?

  (doing this in Welsh whenever possible)

- question or drill the pupils randomly?
  (to ensure that the majority LISTEN to and concentrate on peer contributions)

- permit mistakes to be made within a safe environment?
  (to promote pupil confidence and encourage risk-taking)

- display an awareness of the way in which 'closed' and 'open' questions can affect the teaching?
  (In the former, only one or two word answers are possible: *Ydw / Nac ydw, Oes / Nac oes,* etc. In the latter, pupils are given an opportunity to voice their experience, e.g.

  Beth wyt ti'n hoffi wneud?
  Dw i'n hoffi …

  Pam rwyt ti'n drist?
  Achos …

- set definite time-limits for presentation?
  (in order to quickly progress to language use)

- provide sufficient oral examples before commencing an activity?
  (e.g. by performing a dialogue or a partner/group game with members of the class to ensure that everyone is familiar with the work which is to be undertaken)

- use suitable and attractive resources to facilitate the presentation?
  (e.g. puppets, props, pictures, videoclips, etc.)
  (For a more detailed discussion of the options available see **Addysg Gymraeg – Addysg Gymreig** (Roberts/Williams, Prifysgol Cymru, Bangor, 2003) pp. 238-261.)

3. SETTING UP AN ACTIVITY

WHY?
- to teach/learn and practise new language items
- to get rid of common errors/mistakes (either as a class or a group)
- to practise language
  (e.g. conducting an experiment by copying the language teacher's steps)

WHEN?
- following or during a presentation

THINGS TO CONSIDER
Has the trainee teacher:
- ensured that the pupils have a clear model?
- ascertained that the **meaning** of the language is understood?
- demonstrated the **exact activity** with member(s) of the class?
- asked a pair/group to demonstrate the intended activity?
- ascertained that the pupils know exactly what they have to do (and why)?

- created a **meaningful** activity – which usually entails the use of an information gap?

  (this simply means that the person asking the question does not know the answer to it before asking the question)

- been more than willing to accept any pupil suggestions?

  (e.g. Children: *Sut ydych chi'n dweud* 'it's boring', Miss?)

- given ample time for the pupils to undertake the work?
- moved about the class to stimulate, support and note any examples of 'good practice'?

NOTE

Teachers sometimes refer to a 'drill' rather than an 'activity'. In practice, an open drill (where an information gap exists) can often be synonymous with what others would deem to be an activity.

4. DRILLING

WHY?

- to correct/get rid of common errors/mistakes (either as a class or group)
- to teach/learn new language items
- to practise language

WHEN?

- during presentation or revision

THINGS TO CONSIDER

Does the trainee teacher:

- ensure that the pupils pronounce clearly and speak naturally, imitating intonation and tone?
- keep the initial drill simple and brief, extending gradually?
- ascertain that the pupils UNDERSTAND the meaning of the language?

  (e.g. by explaining the meaning in English before repeating in Welsh 2 or 3 times – *Mae hi'n neidio* – She's jumping.

  Mae hi'n neidio. Mae hi'n neidio … or using flash cards or mime, instead of English, to confirm the meaning)

- progress from class to group or individual drills?
- sometimes ask the pupils to conduct the drilling?
- accept pupil suggestions?

  (e.g. Teacher: *Mae'n … dda/ofnadwy/sothach*

  Children: *Mae'n … boring/grêt*)

- drill in a rapid and slick manner?
- use good pupils to drill a group alongside the teacher?
- use good responses as models for weaker pupils?
- use simple substitution and extension (changing or adding one element at a time)?

  (e.g. *Mae hi'n/ Mae o/e'n … fach/swil/ddel/bert/hapus.*

  Mae hi'n fach ac yn swil.

  Dydy hi ddim yn fach nac yn swil).

- Switch seamlessly from closed drills to information gap drills?

  (i.e. by talking and asking questions naturally e.g. *Ydy hi'n swil/ Ydy o/e'n hapus?*)

NOTE

It is important that the trainee teachers gradually learn to *conceal* the drilling process by e.g. using story telling techniques, playing a game or using songs or verses in which repetition naturally occurs.

5. CLASSROOM ORGANISATION

WHY?

- to teach the pupils to COMMUNICATE

  (e.g. **Pair work** provides more time for individuals to have oral practice than group or class work)

- to ensure variety and flexibility in the teaching

  (e.g. to ensure that the pupils do not tire of practising before being allowed to put the language to use.
  Pair/group work can imperceptibly foster confidence in language use. Help can be proffered to **individuals** without this being obvious)

- to interweave the language skills

For example:			Formative assessment
LISTENING	to a story on tape	individual work	possible
READING	the story aloud	group work	possible
ORAL WORK	characterising part of the story	pair work	possible
WRITING	scripting part of the story	individual/pair work	possible
PERFORMING	part of the story	pair work	oral assessment
DISCUSSING	the story/performance	whole class/group work	monitoring

WHEN?

- regularly

  (although lessons may be developed in many ways, combining two, three or all of the above is the key to the successful organisation of a language class)

THINGS TO CONSIDER

Does the trainee teacher:

- display an awareness of the activities which lend themselves to pair or group work?
- prepare the pupils thoroughly, providing a supportive framework?
  (be it for oral, reading or written work)
- display an awareness of the link between the type of group employed and the requirements of the task?
- circulate during the pair/group work providing assistance, making discreet suggestions, encouraging pupils to elaborate, etc?

OPPORTUNITIES for PAIR WORK

To:

- practise newly-presented dialogues using questions and answers
- express personal experiences
  (Beth wyt ti'n fwyta i frecwast?
  Dw i'n bwyta tost a marmalêd)
- play 'information gap' games (See the Appendix)
- create, practise, mime, and perform dialogues

OPPORTUNITIES for GROUP WORK

To:

- play board games
  (in many games participants can gather their thoughts while others are 'playing')

- ask questions, get answers and arrive at a conclusion
  (e.g. finding out what everyone in the group likes or hates)

- adapt a script for role-play
- record a dialogue/short script.

INDIVIDUAL WORK
THINGS TO CONSIDER

Does the trainee teacher:

*   display an awareness of the activities which lend themselves to individual or class work?
*   display an ability to create a safe, supportive learning environment for individual work?
    (e.g. by setting work that is neither too difficult nor too easy, by praising, smiling, etc.)

*   get the pupils to respond individually (with acceptable pronunciation and intonation), and to question and respond to each other with increasing confidence?
    (e.g. by means of a questionnaire)

*   prepare reading and writing tasks (at an appropriate language level) that will enable the pupils to succeed and to learn?
*   pay attention to shy individuals so that everyone is treated equally?
*   permit and encourage individuals to enquire, seek an explanation or make a remark in Welsh of their own volition?

For instance the following responses could be expected at the levels shown:

LEVEL 1	LEVEL 2
Ble mae'r pyped? *Ga i beintio?*	*Mae … yn sâl heddiw* (at registration) *Rwy/Dw i'n hoffi canu.*
LEVEL 3	**LEVEL 4**
Rwy/Dw i wedi gorffen (on completing a writing task) *Mae siwmper newydd (gy)da fi* *Ydyn ni'n mynd i'r neuadd?*	*Mae gen i siwmper newydd* *Mae'n gas gen i siopa efo Mam* *Mae'n gas (gy)da fi siopa (gy)da Mam*

Does the trainee teacher:

- get everyone in the class to join in an activity or game?

  (e.g. a game to revise vocabulary, to reinforce language patterns, to describe and give directions. See the Appendix)

- ensure that there is sufficient time for some of the pairs/groups to report back – to give the others an opportunity to practise listening (and suggest changes/improvements)?

  (Being sensitive to individual feelings is important in this context)

- succeed in getting the rest of the class to question pupils who have 'performed'?

  (e.g. about a role played by them)

LEVEL 2	LEVEL 3
Ble wyt ti'n byw, Sali Mali?	*Beth ydy/yw enw dy ffrind, Batman?*

6. MOTIVATING PUPILS TO ENQUIRE/ASK QUESTIONS

WHY?
- to enable pupils to initiate conversations
- to promote confidence
- to make speaking a language an active experience

WHEN?
- from the outset

THINGS TO CONSIDER

Has the trainee teacher:

- ensured that the pupils have sufficient language to formulate questions?

  (e.g. Has the following been presented in class: *Beth ydy* 'mountain' *yn Gymraeg?*)

- ensured that the pupils have ample opportunities to ask questions?
- ensured that the atmosphere is relaxed enough for pupils to venture to enquire?

7. REPORTING BACK AND RECEIVING FEEDBACK

WHY?
- to 'gather in' the work of the class (or group) at the end of an activity
- to enable the teacher to draw attention to good practice
- to provide weaker pupils with a model to which they can aspire
- to give pupils confidence
- to provide an opportunity for the trainee teacher to ask for alternative ways of expression

WHEN?
- at the end of every activity
- when there is a need to provide a model for weaker pupils
- when there is a need to draw attention to good practice

THINGS TO CONSIDER
Has the trainee teacher:
- listened to every pair/group?
- tried to note good practice in the work of every pair/group?
- noted any common weaknesses in the work of pairs/groups?
  (for attention in a subsequent lesson)

- noted how pupils could be helped to overcome their weaknesses?

8. CONCLUDING AN ACTIVITY OR LESSON

WHY?
- to draw activities to a neat and purposeful conclusion
- to draw attention to what has been accomplished
- to ensure that the pupils have understood
- to reinforce the main points learned
- to promote confidence

WHEN?
- at the end of each activity
- at the end of each lesson
- at the end of every theme

THINGS TO CONSIDER
Has the trainee teacher:
- drawn attention to what has been accomplished?
- noted who has/has not understood?
- reinforced the main points?
- praised the efforts made?

Section B
Additional Skills

9. VOCABULARY SELECTION

WHY?
- to ensure that the basic vocabulary of a situation (reading material or theme) is taught
- to ensure that the vocabulary is suited to a theme and/or context

WHEN?
- when planning a lesson or series of lessons
- when undertaking any oral/reading/written work
- when dealing orally with pupils in class

THINGS TO CONSIDER
Is the trainee teacher aware:

- of the frequency with which words are normally used?

  [e.g. in the context of FOOD the word *brechdanau* (sandwiches) will be used much more frequently than a word like *madarch* (mushrooms) or *iau/afu* (liver)]

- of the fact that some words are equally useful in several contexts?

  [e.g. the word *gwneud* (to do) has far more uses than a word like *nofio* (to swim)]

- that words can be transferred from one context to another?

  [e.g. **wyneb** *dyn;* **wyneb** *cloc,* **wyneb** *y tir* (a man's face, a clock's face, etc.)]

- that new words can sometimes be learnt by means of the 'old'?

  [e.g. *dau* **wyneb**og, *ar***wyneb**edd (two-faced, surface)]

- that verbs like *mynd, dod, edrych, gwrando*, etc., although rare in one context, may be used quite frequently in general conversation?

- of words that, although not often heard, are vital when we deal with specific contexts?

  [e.g. child/classroom orientated language, etc. – *doli, tedi, bwrdd du, tywod*]

- of the importance of words that provide colour and vitality?

  [e.g. the vocabulary needed to graphically illustrate an experience – or understand a story – such as *bron â llwgu* (famished), … *'am lanast!'* (what a mess!)]

- of the importance of using English and Welsh cognates, especially at the outset?

  [e.g. *jeli, siocled, pys, letus, marmalêd, côt, tei, siwmper, anorac, blows*, etc. In this way a substantial number of words can be rapidly learnt by employing substitution – i.e. changing one element or word – within a pattern: *Dw i'n hoffi … jeli, siocled,* etc. *Mae o/hi'n gwisgo … anorac, blows, siaced, jîns,* etc.]

10. CORRECTING MISTAKES

WHY?
- to ensure that the pupils are given an acceptable model
- to demonstrate the standard to which the pupils should aspire

WHEN?
- when errors cloud the meaning
- when bad practice is in danger of taking root
- when correcting will not undermine pupil confidence
- when it is obvious that the pupils have not understood

THINGS TO CONSIDER
Does the trainee teacher:
- correct items which are going to improve the pupils' communicative abilities?
- correct in an interesting and memorable way?
- correct in a supportive way?
- refrain from correcting **everything** to avoid undermining confidence?
- ensure that only **basic** items are corrected?
- correct *class* errors in an occasional brief, intensive period of teaching?
- try to correct in an unobtrusive manner?

  [e.g. by repeating the question as if it has not been understood, or by giving a correct answer to a question which was asked incorrectly!]
- signify that syntax is more important than remembering every Welsh word?
- display patience – being aware that errors will generally decrease over a period of time?

11. TRANSFERRING LANGUAGE ACROSS CONTEXTS

WHY?
- to prevent a construction from being limited to a single context

  [e.g. Using language patterns – such as **expressing likes/dislikes** – which were presented with 'food' to discuss television programmes, sport, films, hobbies, computer games, etc. Transferring the language of **expressing possession** from 'pets' to clothes, computer games, Pokémon cards, etc.]

WHEN?
- when introducing a new situation
- when moving from one situation to another

THINGS TO CONSIDER
Does the trainee teacher:
- offer opportunities (and encouragement) for pupils to use previously learnt language items in new situations?

  [The term **language items** is used to indicate vocabulary, syntax, phrases, idioms, etc.]
- remember that new vocabulary is usually taught more successfully within familiar constructions (and that new constuctions are usually taught more sucessfully with familiar vocabulary).

12. TEACHER QUESTIONING

Language teachers usually ask questions in different ways, and for differing intentions. The following comments are intended as a very rough guide.

WHY?

- to encourage a response
- to sustain a conversation
- to test understanding
- to make a pupil expand on a statement made, or a question answered, etc.

WHEN?

- regularly, as an integral part of the teaching

THINGS TO CONSIDER

Does the trainee teacher:

- ask questions with which the pupils can readily cope?
- ask 'open' or 'closed' questions? (See page 49)
- know the difference between the 'open' and the 'closed' kind?
- know when each should be employed and for what purpose?

13. EXTENDING CONVERSATIONS

In this context, 'extending' can mean either (i) extending the **length of individual statements** or (ii) extending the **length of a dialogue**.

WHY?

- to eliminate the over-use of one word answers
- to help the pupils to maintain a conversation
- to promote confidence
- to learn the basic craft of sentence building

WHEN?

- when it is felt that the pupils possess sufficient language
- when an opportunity arises to join two simple statements

  [e.g. *Mae John yn dod o Lerpwl <u>ac</u> mae Mary'n dod o Lerpwl hefyd* (See page 59)

  Mae John yn dod o Lerpwl <u>ond</u> mae William yn dod o Manceinion.]

THINGS TO CONSIDER

Does the trainee teacher:

- take advantage of opportunities to contribute to a conversation?

  [The contribution may be based on the truth or be purely imaginative. This will give the impression that the communication is real.]

Example:	Teacher:	*Beth wyt ti'n hoffi bwyta?*
	Pupil:	*Jeli.*
	T:	*Jeli coch, jeli melyn?*
	P:	*Jeli coch.*
	T:	*Ych a fi! Dw i ddim yn hoffi jeli.*
		Ond dw i'n hoffi siocled …
	P:	*A fi.*
	T:	*Siocled gwyn te siocled brown?*
	P:	*Siocled gwyn a brown.*
	T:	*Y ddau?*
	P:	*Y ddau!*

- encourage pupils to extend using **MEMORY-JOGGING** prompts?

  The following would perhaps be used in the above conversation:

Teacher:	*O ble mae John yn dod?*
Pupil:	*Mae John yn dod o Lerpwl.*
T:	**A Mary?**
P:	*Ac mae Mary'n dod o Lerpwl hefyd.*

- encourage pupils to extend using the following questions:

Pryd?	**Pam?**	**Ble?**	**Pwy?**	**Sut?**	**Beth?**	**Sawl?**	**Faint?**	**Faint o?**

Example:		
	Pupil:	*Mae gen i gath.*
	Teacher:	*Faint?*
	P:	*Pump.*
	T:	*Pump! Beth ydy'r enwau (names)?*
		Smot?
	P:	*Percy.*
	T:	*A?*
	P:	*Bertha.*
	T:	*Bertha! Pam Bertha?*
	P:	*Achos enw Mam ydy Bertha.*

Section C
Ways of Enriching Language

14. EVERYDAY WELSH / CYMRAEG POB DYDD

WHY?
- to make Welsh a natural (and integral) part of class activity
- to give a real communicative purpose to learning Welsh
- to take advantage of naturally repetitive classroom situations and/or rituals
  [e.g. *Beth ydy'r dyddiad heddiw? Sut dywydd ydy hi? Byddwch yn dawel. Sefwch wrth y drws.*]

WHEN?
- to 'manage' the daily activities of a class (See grid below)
- to socialise within the class
- to explain specific tasks
- to take advantage of language-developing curricular opportunities

Everyday Welsh can be used:

During	break/snack play art and music	lunch experiments assemblies, services	registration cooking lessons extra-curricular activities	games physical education
To	praise expedite everyday rituals (e.g. the weather, days of the week, months, seasons, years) seek permission	discipline explain	greet / say goodbye display	command instruct, etc

THINGS TO CONSIDER
Is the trainee teacher's use of *Cymraeg Pob Dydd:*
- a natural, integral part of classroom life?
- carefully woven into every lesson plan?
- appropriately adapted to the learners' level of proficiency?
- comprehensible, so that individuals, as well as groups (or the whole class), can respond correctly either verbally or non-verbally?
  Is it:
- regularly used in real situations?
- clearly displayed?
  [so that those who may need it can easily refer to it. See 'Displaying Work', page 74]
- also used naturally by the children?

One effective way of using Welsh in class is to appoint a '**HELPWR HEDDIW**' on a daily basis. The helper's task is to assist with arrangements/rituals which are a part of classroom daily life. An example from Uned 12 *Siarad Cymraeg yn y Dosbarth* (Non ap Emlyn), can be found in the Appendix.

The functions of HELPWR HEDDIW are also discussed in '*The National INSET Programme – Welsh, Aspects of Teaching Welsh as a Second Language in Key Stages 1 and 2*': *Datblygu Cymraeg Pob Dydd yn yr Ysgol Gynradd*.
Ed. Richard Roberts, WJEC (1999), pp.14 -19.

15. USING INFORMATION AND COMMUNICATION TECHNOLOGY (ICT)

WHY?
- to develop (and adapt) the pupils' ICT skills through the medium of Welsh
- to reinforce pupils' understanding and knowledge of Welsh by providing extra practice
- to gather and use information
- to give the work of both pupils and trainee teachers a professional finish
- to give credence and a modern image to the language being learnt
- to communicate with other schools [e.g. by using e-mail]

WHEN?
- whenever computerised material is available to complement the teaching/learning
- during carefully planned sessions
- when there is time to draft/re-draft, etc.

THINGS TO CONSIDER
Does the trainee teacher offer the pupils opportunities to:
- play language games?
- work on their compositions with others?
- create and present their work to a designated audience?
  [e.g. class magazine, letter, etc.]
- research for information?
- use a variety of resource facilities and data-bases?
  [e.g. Clip Art, Compact Discs, the Web, etc.]
- use video and recording apparatus to develop language?
- use computer programmes to promote accuracy?
- be creative?
- record information?
- draft, edit and design?

In addition, does the trainee teacher:
- provide support without being over-intrusive?
- use ICT purposefully?
- use ICT unnecessarily?
- divide the work into manageable portions to ensure success?

WHY?

- to ensure that the language is allowed to develop as a medium
- to give the language learning process a meaningful context
- to bring the real world into language learning
- to prevent pupils from regarding Welsh as a mere subject
- to prevent pupils from associating Welsh with specific lessons (see page 108)

WHEN?

- whenever opportunities arise in the course of the teaching.

  [e.g. (i) in situations where **repetition** naturally occurs, such as experiments;

  (ii) in **concrete** situations, such as the gymnasium, the rugby field, the hall, etc.]

THINGS TO CONSIDER

Has the trainee teacher:

- ensured that he/she has sufficient language to meet the challenge?
- prepared thoroughly?
- chosen a subject (or field) which is comparatively easy for pupils to understand (and remember)?
- chosen a subject (or field) with wide appeal?
- ensured that the content is suitable for the age and ability range being taught?

  [e.g. the following would be suitable for KS2 but **not** for KS1: *Mae coeden yn tyfu. Mae dail ar y coed*, etc.]

- ensured that all possible available resources are being used?

  [e.g. props, pictures, diagrams, puppets, equipment, etc.]

- made the fullest possible use of all the senses?
- chosen a subject (or field) that appeals to both boys and girls?
- made full use of previously taught language in the present context?

  [e.g. *Mae **Dad a Mam** yn byw yn ... Mae **Esgimo** yn byw yn ...*

  *Roedd **Tadcu/Taid** yn gwisgo 'winkle-pickers'. Roedd **Caradog** yn gwisgo tiwnig yn Rhufain.*]

WHY?

- to improve motivation and foster positive attitudes
- to bring variety to the teaching – through the use of a wide range of speakers, situations and techniques
- to authenticate the learning, by:
  - bringing the world into the classroom
  - teaching the pupils to interpret paralinguistic clues
    [e.g. facial expressions, body language, etc. They convey much information and assist comprehension]
- to teach the pupils to respond to contextual clues
- to form a basis for a host of activities – at all language levels

WHEN?

- as a regular part of a varied scheme of work – to present language and/or reinforce the learning context

THINGS TO CONSIDER

Is the trainee teacher:

- familiar with the material available for learners?

For example:

KS1	KS2
'Parablu' HTV Cardiff *'Bobol Bach'* Mid Glamorgan *'Gwyliau George'* HTV Cardiff	*'Clwb Clebran'* HTV Cardiff *'Muzzy'* BBC Cardiff *'Iaith Iau 2'* Mid Glamorgan

- aware of other television material that would be equally suitable?
  [e.g. Clips from children's programmes, 'Pingu', 'Tom and Jerry', 'Mr Bean' (see the Appendix pp. 111-112), soaps like *'Pobol y Cwm'*, etc.]
- able to show that he/she has considered the following during lesson preparation:
  - what should be presented (or done) **before** the viewing
  - how, when and why the clip/programme should be interrupted
  - which activities could be completed during the viewing
  - which suitable activities could follow the viewing experience?

Is the trainee teacher able to:

- select brief rather than extended viewing clips?
- ensure that they match the linguistic capabilities of the pupils?
- ensure that the picture and sound are of the best possible quality?
- ensure that every pupil can see and hear well?
- present any work to be done concisely and clearly?
- set definite unambiguous tasks for the pupils to complete?
  [This ensures that the viewing does not become a passive experience.]

WHY?

*   to sustain pupil interest
*   to connect the language learning with the outside world
*   to introduce the learner to the realms of the imagination
*   to present and reinforce vocabulary and structure
*   to teach the learner to cope with the unexpected
    [the unexpected frequently occurs in everyday speech]
*   to foster confidence in reading, writing and discussion

WHEN?

*   as a starting point to a series of language sessions – or a theme
*   when a story serves to illuminate a theme or experience
*   as a regular developmental component of a varied programme
*   when a vehicle is required to connect a number of random elements

THINGS TO CONSIDER [during **preparation**]

Does the story:

*   provide enjoyment and sustain the pupils' interest?
*   correspond to the pupils' developmental and linguistic levels?
*   repeat appropriate vocabulary and language patterns?
*   include enough familiar vocabulary and patterns?
*   contain attractive illustrations and clues that manifest the meaning?
*   contain short, self-standing, lively and interesting episodes?
*   appear attractive and clear in plan and presentation?
*   promote the learners' ability to anticipate and predict?

THINGS TO CONSIDER [when **presenting** or telling a class story]

Does the trainee teacher:

*   prepare the pupils for the story by introducing/revising the story's key vocabulary and/or patterns?
*   make use of suitable aids to elicit the meaning?
    [e.g. puppets, toys, masks, flash cards, etc.]
*   ensure that the classroom organisation facilitates listening?
*   ensure that the print and illustrations are clearly seen?
*   read the story to the class using effective pronunciation, intonation and characterisation?
*   when re-reading the story, encourage the pupils to participate, whenever they wish?
*   draw attention to language items in ways which:
    *   reinforce understanding
    *   extend knowledge and interest?
        [e.g. through question and discussion]
*   provide opportunities for pupils to listen to recorded stories (that use a variety of voices and sound effects) and follow them in text?
*   plan subsequent, relevant activities – which interweave reading, oral work and writing?

NOTE

Not all the above are relevant to **presenting** a story. They should, however, be borne in mind when planning a 'lesson'.

Section D
Reading and Writing

19. READING

WHY?

*   to provide pleasure and enjoyment
*   to reinforce language that is orally familiar
*   to extend vocabulary
*   to strengthen pupils' language resources
*   to gather information
*   to stimulate an oral and/or written response
*   to maintain interest

WHEN?

The written word plays a central role in language learning. Reading should therefore occur (to some degree) in every 'lesson'

*   The specific teaching of reading should be planned within a cohesive programme which integrates oracy, reading and writing.

THINGS TO CONSIDER

Does the trainee teacher:

*   select factual and fictional material that is suited to the pupils' developmental and linguistic levels?

    [It is important to remember that reading material can be adapted and simplified by e.g. changing a text from the past to the present, or using *gwneud* to obviate the use of the short past tense forms of the verb – '*Mi welodd y gath y ci*'; '*Mi wnaeth y gath weld y ci*'/*Mi ddaru'r gath weld y ci*', etc. Although using *gwneud* as an auxilliary verb may appear difficult, it is the only construction needed to convey the past]

*   prepare the pupils before reading or presenting a story?
    e.g. by
    *   discussing the context without revealing too much of the plot
    *   discussing familiar language items
    *   getting the pupils to guess the meaning of key words and phrases
    *   explaining key words and phrases when that is necessary
    *   introducing a handout noting the key vocabulary
    *   talking about the illustrations
    *   directing the pupils to reference books and/or dictionaries
    *   making use of video/audio tapes to accompany the text, etc.

- promote comprehension? e.g. by:
  - displaying the language being read within the classroom [in the form of murals, posters, signs, flash cards, etc.]
  - ensuring that the reading reinforces the oral and written work
  - drawing the pupils' attention to clues which can aid comprehension [e.g. pictures, headings, punctuation, context, etc]
  - reminding pupils that a text can be enjoyed (and understood) without knowing every word

- teach the pupils how to read aloud to others?
  e.g. by:
  - practising a dialogue or play with a partner or fellow group member
  - reading individual words or sentences from the classroom walls
  - reading quotations from a book created in the classroom
  - reading each other's creations
  - recording a story/dialogue with a partner on a sound or video tape

- get the pupils to respond to their reading through oral work?
  e.g. by
  - discussing the subject matter of a book/story/article/letter − using such questions as:
    Ydych chi'n gallu ... ? Ydych chi'n hoffi ... ?
    Ydy o/hi'n drist/ hapus/gas ... ?
    Ydyn nhw wedi bod yn ... ?
    Pwy sy ... ? Beth sy ... ?
  - and using terms like *plot, awdur, drama, sgript, pennill,* etc. (at **Level 4**)
  - using the passage / poem read as a basis for role-play
  - using drama
    [e.g. getting groups to act out parts of a story during Assembly]
  - miming or drawing pictures to a read description

- get the pupils to respond to their reading with written tasks?
  e.g. by
  - responding to a letter
  - creating simple scripts using characters from a book
  - writing reviews
  - filling in questionnaires
  - creating a class book based on a familiar story

- get the pupils to read independently and enjoy the experience?
  e.g. by
  - discussing recently acquired new books in class
  - ensuring vocabulary and language pattern support
  - reading big books / class books together, before ensuring opportunities for personal reading
  - creating opportunities for pupils to read each other's work.

- The text and context can be clearly seen while the trainee teacher is reading. The pupils can then model themselves on the fluent reader
- It allows a group of pupils to interact with the book, with each other and/or with the trainee teacher
- The illustration(s) on each page can be discussed before asking the pupils to point to the words as the trainee teacher reads
- Since the pupils are reading together there is less stigma attached to a failure to read a word
- The pupils read by 'following' the 'pointer'
- The emphasis is on reading for enjoyment and meaning rather than on the analysis of words, although that aspect will also be developed simultaneously
- During the reading process pupils possessing different skills will help each other
- Pupils can read 'big books' together without the help of the teacher
- They provide opportunities to develop and extend oral proficiency (whilst discussing the story) especially when pupils are allowed to respond individually and share ideas
- 'Big books' can be used for paired reading work or to get older pupils to read to younger children

WHY?

*   to reinforce oral and reading work
*   to offer opportunities for concentration and contemplation
    [Written work forces the pupils to use more accurate language]
*   to bring more variety into classroom activities

WHEN?

*   as an integral part of a programme that combines listening, oral, reading and writing activities naturally and skilfully.
    (The main emphasis will naturally be on **oral** work)

THINGS TO CONSIDER

Does the trainee teacher:

*   set interesting tasks?
*   set tasks which reinforce and develop pupil proficiency?
*   set tasks that are based on reading and/or oral/listening activities?
*   use a **variety** of writing activities?
    [See the Appendix]
*   show an awareness of the developmental stages of the writing process?
    [See: p.69]
*   ensure that everyone understands what is to be done?
    [e.g. by using printed aids such as a list of the vocabulary/phrases already introduced, supportive frameworks relevant to the task, features of the *genre* being used – letter, diary, postcard, etc.]
*   give written work pride of place and afford it value?
    [e.g. by
    *   displaying it tastefully
    *   composing class booklets on specific themes or topics
    *   encouraging the pupils to 'perform' their written work
    *   encouraging the pupils to write to a 'real' audience – for example letters to thank a visitor, letters to pupils at other schools, invitations to friends, letters to Welsh magazines, etc.]
*   use computers regularly (and purposefully) to enable pupils to re-draft and polish their work?

A competent trainee teacher will mark in a positive manner – by:
- ignoring some mistakes in order to concentrate on others
- asking the pupils to re-draft
- encouraging them to correct some elements themselves
  [this can be done with groups as well as individuals]
- having noted the strengths and weaknesses of the pupils' work, basing future teaching units on that information.

During such lessons, the trainee teacher will ask himself/herself such questions as:
- Should I stop here for a while?
- What must I present **again**?
- Are they ready to move on? etc.

THE DEVELOPMENTAL STEPS OF THE WRITING PROCESS★

1. Copying	words, sentences, phrases, etc.
2. Reproducing	re-creating copied work from memory
3. Recombining	creating new combinations by drawing on steps 1 &2
4. Writing within a supportive framework	following a framework e.g. recording personal details within a template letter
5. Free composition	

- Step 4 will be extensively used to develop writing, but even at this stage the trainee teacher will often return to preceding steps, according to pupil needs. When appropriate he/she will also venture forward to Step 5.
- The trainee teacher (or pupil) will often combine a number of steps within an activity.

  ★ (The steps are based on Wilga Rivers: **'A Practical Guide to the Teaching of English as a Second or Foreign Language'**, OUP, 1978).

KEY STAGE 1

- labelling pictures and objects
- writing words in 'bubbles'
- filling in simple questionnaires and graphs
- making posters using familiar language
- writing simple sentences

  [e.g. news – picture and sentence, recording personal experiences, etc]

- completing work sheets
- creating greeting cards, cards for special occasions, etc.
- writing simple letters

  [e.g. to thank Father Christmas or accept an invitation to a party, etc.]

- creating a shopping list, lists of favourite foods, games, videos, clothes, etc.

KEY STAGE 2

The teacher reinforces and develops what was learnt in KS1 by adding activities such as the following:

- devising menus
- recording recipes
- giving directions
- creating simple maps
- making charts/timetables
- creating short biographies of modern celebrities
- keeping diaries
- creating news/weather bulletins, etc.
- creating simple advertisements
- filling in grids [e.g. based on reading a simple information pamphlet]
- creating information charts [e.g. dealing with fire/caring for teeth]
- creating simple books for younger children
- creating rules
- creating warnings
- creating a family tree – real or imaginary
- devising plans [e.g. for houses, sports centres, schools, etc.]
- writing invitations [e.g. to a wedding, party, etc.]
- creating a cartoon strip
- creating short dialogues
- substituting words within a dialogue
- extending dialogues
- completing one half of a dialogue
- completing or creating simple word-searches
- writing messages
- filling in Cloze gaps
- devising Trivial Pursuit questions, etc.

NOTE

Teachers should offer pupils ample opportunities to use WORD PROCESSORS – to create, redraft, correct and design during both Key Stages.

Section E
Other Resources and Techniques

21. ROLE-PLAY

WHY?
- to develop the ability to communicate in real situations
- to practise and/or reinforce specific language items
- to provide support – as pupils learn to socialise, express needs, give and provide information, protest, persuade, etc.
- to encourage the pupils to be inventive, confident and creative

WHEN?
- when the context lends itself to this kind of activity
- as a regular part of a varied activity-based programme

THINGS TO CONSIDER
(i) Has the trainee teacher ensured that the role play or dialogue:
- is short enough to be learnt and performed in one or two sessions?
- uses sufficient familiar language to allow the pupils to listen and understand with relative ease?
- includes sufficient new language to extend the pupils' 'proficiency'?
- reflects the pupils' interests and/or communicative needs?
  [In this context, features like humour, interjections, natural everyday phrases, etc. are very important.]
- provides a clear and concise model for ensuing written tasks?
- is structured? [so that **all** the pupils can enjoy a measure of success]

(ii) Were the pupils given enough opportunities to:
- adapt existing dialogues to new situations?
- practise information/knowledge gap role-play?
  [i.e. where B conveyed information that was new to A]
- play roles that would prepare them for natural conversations?
  [e.g. teaching them how to begin a conversation, to respond, to agree, to disagree, etc.]

(iii) Were suitable resources available to reinforce the teaching?
  [e.g. sentence strips, pictures, 'props', suitable locations, etc.]
(iv) Did the trainee teacher circulate to offer support?
(v) Was sufficient time allowed for the pupils to practise?
(vi) Was sufficient time allowed for the pupils to 'perform'?
(vii) Was sufficient time allowed for the pupils to receive feedback?

1. Teachers often begin role-play work with ready-made dialogues – which combine language previously learnt within a meaningful context. **A** (in the Appendix: page 139) exemplifies some of the teacher's considerations when preparing such a script. **B** and **C** are further examples of similar work.

    D is an example of role-play which can be undertaken – without a script – with an infant class. In such work there will be much imitation and playing with dolls and puppets.

2. A measure of support is frequently needed on the road to free expression. The kind of support offered can be seen in example **E**. In such work carefully selected (teacher) constructions are combined with pupil options. In **F** and **G** flash cards are used for support and as memory prompts.

3. Preparing a 'free' dialogue can signify more than one thing:
    *   an entirely **extempore** conversation
    *   a script-free 'performance' following group/pair practice
    *   a 'performance' based on loose scripting, etc.

4. The ability to play a role (or perform a dialogue) based on 'information gaps' is not an activity to be reserved for the advanced learner. As seen in **D**, it can be a part of the learning process from a very early stage.

    [Where an **'information gap'** exists a speaker gives his/her partner information which the partner did not previously know.]

22. BOARD / CLASS GAMES

The games used to teach and practise language may either be commercial ones (e.g. *Guess Who* or the WJEC Language Games pack) or games that teachers have devised for use with their pupils.

WHY?
*   to entertain whilst intensively practising language items
    [e.g. vocabulary; asking and answering questions; speaking in complete sentences; reading comprehension practice; conveying information, etc.]
*   to provide pupils with opportunities to communicate with each other

WHEN?
*   usually after a whole class presentation
*   as a regular and DEVELOPMENTAL part of a varied scheme of work

THINGS TO CONSIDER
Has the trainee teacher ensured:
*   that the rules are easy to learn?
*   that the competition is not too intense?
*   that there is sufficient competition to produce excitement?

- that the game corresponds to the language level of the pupils?
- that on occasions there is competition between teams (as well as between individuals)?
- that the majority of the participants can achieve a measure of success?
- that SPEAKING IN WELSH is essential to play the game?
- that before play is commenced the language and rules of the game have been thoroughly learnt?

23. FLASH CARDS

WHY?
- to introduce vocabulary

  [so that pupils can **see** as well as hear a word]
- to reinforce language patterns using cartoons, signs, etc.

  [e.g. *dw i ddim yn hoffi*]
- to prompt language activity
- to obviate the need for translation and/or the mother tongue
- to jog the memory

WHEN?
- regularly during presentation, language activities and revision

THINGS TO CONSIDER
Do the flashcards:
- isolate the point to be learnt?
- convey their message clearly and unambiguously?
- help rather than hinder pupil comprehension?
- have a consistent style, as far as possible?
- come between the learner and the message to be conveyed?

> 'In teaching a new word, linguistic pattern or situation, a suitable picture can teach, in two seconds, that which could not have been achieved by many minutes of verbal explanation'
>
> Cennard Davies

24. PICTURES / ILLUSTRATIONS

WHY?
- to provide a basis for role play and story telling
- to stimulate a question/answer session
- to enliven proceedings
- to jog the memory
- to maintain pupil interest
- to convey meaning

WHEN?

- when engaged in role play and story-based activities, etc.
- on occasions, to effect a change of person – *Mae o/hi/nhw*, etc.
- to take advantage of the wealth of information which an illustration can convey
- to discuss the concrete (that which **is**) and the hypothetical/imaginary (that which **could happen**)
- to change tense from the present to the past or to the future, etc.

THINGS TO CONSIDER

Do the illustrations
- fulfil the requirements of the lesson?

    (i.e. is the trainee teacher able to control the content so as to concentrate on the relevant language items?)
- highlight the point to be learned?
- convey a clear unambiguous message?
- help rather than hinder pupil understanding?
- stimulate conversation and discussion?
- do no more than serve as a mere decoration?

25. DISPLAYING WORK

WHY?

- to celebrate pupil achievement
- to foster confidence
- to reflect and support the language work
- to stimulate the pupils to enquire and ask questions

WHEN?

- regularly

THINGS TO CONSIDER

Has the trainee teacher ensured that:
- part of the classroom is associated with the Welsh language?

    (e.g. with wall displays, reading corner, puppet theatre, masks, shop, café, etc.)
- the material displayed corresponds to the pupils' linguistic requirements?
    For example:

    (i)   a collage or mural – displaying relevant vocabulary and structures, etc. – on a current theme

    (ii)   vocabulary lists, common patterns and supportive frameworks to which pupils can refer when responding orally or in writing
- the pupils can understand and discuss the work displayed?
- the display area is shared by both pupil and trainee teacher?
- the work is easy to see and read?
- the work displayed is attractive, colourful, and large enough to create an effect?
- the work displayed is not overburdened with language?

WHY?

- to teach new language items
- to extend vocabulary and structures
- to revise and/or reinforce language previously learnt
- for whole class teaching
- to enable pupils to interact with material under teacher supervision
- to stimulate oral/written responses (e.g. scripting, creating dialogues, role play, etc.)
- to provide a 'Big Book' experience
- to bring books to life
- to give language teaching a modern, contemporay image
- to maintain interest

WHEN?

- regularly as an integral part of the teaching
- when suitable material exists

THINGS TO CONSIDER

Does the trainee teacher:

- make full use of the facility?

  (e.g. when Pip (see below) appears on screen the pupils could be asked to name the clothes he is wearing, their colours, etc. The colours could then be changed before the pupil's eyes! They could even be asked to choose their favourite colour, etc)

- make passive use of the facility?

  (by, for example, doing nothing more than playing the programme, without attempting to engage the pupils in any interaction)

- promote active learning?

  (e.g. by questioning the pupils, changing the images on screen, inviting the pupils to make suggestions and/or question peers, jumping from the screen experience into real life, etc.)

NOTE

1. The following materials are available for use at KS2: *Stabec*, *Bobol Bach*, *Pip*, *Ben Bwgan Brain* . Some units could also be used with KS1 pupils. For more information see: www.learn-ict.org.uk

2. All units dealing with oracy, reading and writing are equally applicable to the White Board context.

Section F
Assesment and Appraisal

FOREWORD
Trainee teachers following a B.Ed. course will
i.   appraise themselves
ii.   be appraised by tutors and mentors, and
iii.   assess pupil progress

27. SELF APPRAISAL

WHY?
*   to become aware of the fact that language teachers need to be constantly alert
*   to enable the trainee teacher to make his/her own 'discoveries'

WHEN?
*   after each teaching session

THINGS TO CONSIDER
The aim of the Self Appraisal Sheet (**A**) is to enable the trainee teacher to become self-critical. The questions are meant to be used after each teaching session. (Of course, it will not be necessary to ask **all** the questions every single time!). The process should enable the reasons why some things work and why some do not to become increasingly apparent.

A. SELF APPRAISAL INVENTORY

- Did I relate the *'lesson'* material to previous work?
- Was there a *specific aim* to the lesson?
- Was the lesson material *suitable* for the pupils?
- Did I *present* the new material concisely and clearly?
- Did I *explain* things adequately?
- Did the *starting point* of the lesson stimulate the pupils?
- Were there signs that everyone understood or that some did not?
- Was the lesson material interesting?
- Did I *stimulate* the pupils to respond orally?
- Was the language I used too difficult or too easy?
- Were the activities I used suitable to the lesson aims?
- Did I pay the same attention to everyone when pair/group work was in progress?
- Did I draw the class's attention to *good practice* (i.e. to pupil creations heard when observing the pair/group activity)?
- Did I succeed in capitalising on the pupils' suggestions?
- Did I talk too much?
- Did I talk enough?
- Did I give sufficient encouragement?
- Did the lesson have a purposeful, definite structure?
- Were there adequate links between the different parts of the lesson?
- Was there enough *variety* (with regard to activities/organisation, etc.) within the 'lesson'?
- Did I pay equal attention to all the *language skills*? Or was there too much writing or oral work?
- Did I try to do too much work?
- Did I attempt sufficient work?
- Did I *time* things well?
- Did I capitalise on opportunities offered by the material?
- Did I run short of material/ideas/steam before the end of the lesson?
- Did I succeed in doing everything I had intended?
- Did I take too much for granted?
- Did I *underline* the important things that had been learned?
- Did I draw things together at the end of the lesson?

A SUMMARY OF THE TRAINEE LANGUAGE TEACHER'S SYLLABUS

Trainee Teacher Handouts 1 and 2 (**B** and **C**) are an inventory of the language teaching skills that should become increasingly familiar during the B.Ed. degree course. They are relevant for teaching at either **Key Stage 1** (Levels 1 and 2) (**B**) and/or **Key Stage 2** (Levels 3 and 4) (**C**).

ENCOURAGE THE PUPILS TO:
- take an interest in the work and enjoy it
- work at an appropriate speed
- make mistakes within a safe environment
- use the language with confidence

WITH THE GREAT MAJORITY:
- watching and listening carefully
- responding non-verbally and/or orally.

Trainee teachers should also be able to:
- provide support for reading and writing tasks

- use imaginative ways of questioning, revising and substituting to enable the children to give SLIGHTLY VARIED RESPONSES e.g.

L1: REVISION: vocabulary and familiar patterns:
Put pictures of animals in a 'trailer':- Dyma'r ci/Dyma'r ceffyl, etc.
Ga i iâr os gweluch yn dda?
Ble mae'r gath?
Yn y trelar, etc.

L2: SUBSTITUTION:
using a story and pictures:
Mae Bili Broga yn y llyn/wrth y goeden/dan y ddeilen/o flaen y tŷ
QUESTIONING
Ble mae ... ? Ydy ... ?
Oes ... ?

- use CYMRAEG POB DYDD, adapted to the learners' level, e.g. to praise, greet, talk about the weather, days of the week, register, head for home, bid farewell, command, play games, etc.
- ensure that CYMRAEG POB DYDD is understood by e.g. using the best pupils to exemplify, suggesting, using gestures, etc.
- hold planned sessions on specific language items, etc.
- ensure that the language learnt is actively used by the children e.g by using the 'Helpwr Heddiw'. (See page 61)

---

prepare the children thoroughly to play BOARD/GROUP GAMES, ACT OUT DIALOGUES, PLAY A ROLE and provide sufficient opportunity for them to play/perform, e.g.
GAME: Sut wyt ti? (response based on flash cards)
Du i'n sâl/Go lew, gweddol, etc.

Dialogue: (With Information gap)
Child 1: Wyt ti'n hoffi ____?
Child 2: Ydw. Wyt ti'n hoffi ____?
Child 1: Ych a fi, nac ydw.
Child 2: Wyt ti'n hoffi ____?
Ydw, iym, iym!

Role-play: Imitate the trainee teacher in the Tŷ Bach Twt
Imitate a conversation from a familiar story

Those assessing your work will use the following grade descriptions:

1. VERY GOOD
2. GOOD
3. SATISFACTORY
4. UNSATISFACTORY
5. POOR

THE ESSENTIALS OF GOOD TEACHING LEVELS 1 AND 2 L1/L2

- ASSESS in order to
  - track progress
  - deal with weaknesses

- SELF APPRAISE

PRACTISE LANGUAGE by e.g.:
- using new vocabulary with familiar language patterns.
- drilling 'playfully' e.g. keeping it brief and simple at first and extending gradually
Mae Magi Ann yn dawnsio/peintio
Ydi Magi Ann yn ____?
Ydi/Nac ydi.
- SINGING/RAP/CLASS GAMES – all containing repetition to reinforce the language

---

CONCLUDE lessons effectively e.g. by giving
- sufficient time for revision
- suitable feedback for activities

PLAN effectively

ORGANISE whole class, pair and group work effectively

- use SUITABLE, ATTRACTIVE RESOURCES e.g. stimuli of various kinds

VISUAL	AUDIO-VISUAL	PHYSICAL	SENSORY (TOUCH/SMELL/TASTE)
flash cards	sound tapes	simple actions	pupil activities – appropriate in such contexts as FOOD or activities with a 'feel' box
pictures/books	video clips	action songs	
board games	computer programmes	mime	
computer games	teacher characterisations	games in the round	
masks/puppets	songs/phone calls		
toys			
object box			

Choose a combination of stimuli to PRESENT language, to encourage the CHILDREN TO RESPOND and to PROMOTE an ACTIVITY e.g. to combine the following to present and develop a situation

L1: Feelings cards –
Sut wyt ti? Wedi blino/
Du i'n hapus / Du i'n drist.

Use mime, a class game,
simple story (read), song, video clip
(Parablu)
all based on the above language

L2: Revise clothes vocabulary with flash cards using a puppet, voice characterisation. Introduce – Mae gen i gôt, etc. Sing to a familiar tune –
Oes gen ti siwmper/Oes siwmper 'da ti?
Oes, yn y dôs.
Use a clothes box –
Oes gen ti ____/Oes ____ 'da ti?
Oes, mae gen i ____/Oes, mae ____ 'da fi.

- get the children to PRONOUNCE, MIMIC, and INTONE effectively as a whole class, in groups, individually. Use the printed word, repetition, exaggeration or emphasis to illustrate a variety of intonations.

- ensure that the LISTENING, ORAL, READING and WRITING WORK is INTERDEPENDENT e.g. by
- displaying printed resources, phrases and sentences as well as individual words
- using computer programmes
- choosing attractive, reading material, containing repetition, which will also sustain interest

READ a story → undertake related ORAL work → LISTEN to a sound tape of the same → WRITE a word or two in a 'bubble' or in the form of a sentence and picture based on the story.

THE ESSENTIALS OF GOOD TEACHING LEVELS 3 AND 4 L3/L4

Those assessing your work will use the following grade descriptions:

1. VERY GOOD
2. GOOD
3. SATISFACTORY
4. UNSATISFACTORY
5. POOR

ENCOURAGE THE PUPILS TO:
- take an interest in the work and enjoy it
- work at an appropriate speed
- make mistakes within a safe environment
- use the language with confidence

WITH THE GREAT MAJORITY:
- watching and listening carefully
- responding non-verbally and/or orally.
Trainee teachers should also be able to:
- provide support for reading and writing tasks

- Use imaginative, structured methods to VARY AND INCREASE the pupils' response using :

  Ble? Beth? Sut? Pryd? Pwy? etc.

- Use familiar contexts (e.g. classroom situations, children's interests) and humour to stimulate conversation which will include some voluntary statements [Level 3] and own personal ideas [Level 4].

- use CYMRAEG POB DYDD – adapted to the learners' level, e.g. to praise, greet, talk about the weather, days of the week, register, head for home, bid farewell, command, play games, etc.
- ensure that CYMRAEG POB DYDD is understood by e.g. using the best pupils to exemplify, suggesting, using gestures, etc.
- hold planned sessions on specific language items, etc.
- ensure that the language learnt is actively used by the children e.g by using the 'Helpwr Heddiw'. (See page 61)

- prepare the children thoroughly to play BOARD/ GROUP GAMES, ACT OUT DIALOGUES, PLAY A ROLE and provide sufficient opportunity for them to play/perform, e.g.

Group/class GAME – find a partner with the same information on a card:
Ble/Pryd mae'r disgo? Faint o'r gloch? Faint mae'n gostio?
DIALOGUE (pairs) – Oes gen ti (chwaer) / Oes (chwaer) 'da ti? Oes mae gen i (chwaer) / Oes, mae (chwaer) 'da fi.
Nac oes, ond mae gen i (frawd) / Nac oes, ond mae (brawd) 'da fi. (teulu, eiddo, anifeiliaid anwes)

ROLE-PLAY – 'A policeman and eye-witnesses'
- Offer language opportunities such as varying questions, time, adjectives and commands, etc.

- ASSESS in order to
  - track progress
  - deal with weaknesses

- SELF APPRAISE

PRACTISE AN INCREASING RANGE OF LANGUAGE by e.g.:

- using new vocabulary with familiar language patterns.
- drilling by substituting the words denoted ★
  Roedd e/o★ yn chwarae golff★ ddydd Sadwrn★
- transferring a pattern from one situation to another
  Roedd hi'n mynd i + locations/ countries
- SINGING/RAP/PAIR WORK/CLASS GAMES, telling a STORY – all containing repetition to reinforce the language.

CONCLUDE lessons effectively e.g. by giving
- sufficient time for revision
- suitable feedback to activities

PLAN effectively

ORGANISE whole class, pair and group work effectively

- use SUITABLE, ATTRACTIVE RESOURCES e.g. stimuli of various kinds

VISUAL	AUDIO-VISUAL	PHYSICAL	SENSORY (TOUCH/SMELL/TASTE)
flash cards pictures/books board games computer games masks/puppets toys object box	sound tapes video clips computer programmes teacher characterisations songs/phone calls	simple actions action songs mime games in the round	pupil activities – appropriate in such contexts as FOOD or activities with a 'feel' box

---

- choose a combination of stimuli to PRESENT language, to encourage the CHILDREN TO RESPOND and to PROMOTE ACTIVITY

e.g. – prepare a simple map with children's names in appropriate places. Ask a partner: Ydy Ann yn croesi'r bont/Saul badigen sy'n pasio'r siop? Oes dwy ferch wrth yr eglwys? etc.
- prepare PICTURES (with plenty of action in them) for a question/answer session or GROUP DISCUSSION.
- select VIDEO CLIPS (with various voices on them) suitable to the language level – to reinforce the class work.

- get the children to PRONOUNCE, MIMIC and INTONE effectively, using an increasing range of vocabulary and language patterns, as a whole class, in groups, individually. Use the printed word, repetition, exaggeration or emphasis to illustrate a variety of intonations.

- ensure that the LISTENING, ORAL, READING and WRITING WORK is INTERDEPENDENT e.g. by
- displaying printed resources, phrases and sentences as well as individual words
- using computer programmes
- choosing attractive reading material, containing repetition, which will will also sustain interest

---

READ a story → undertake related ORAL work → LISTEN to a sound tape of the same → WRITE basic sentences, based on the story using suitable vocabulary and varying patterns.

- During each teaching practice period the college **tutor** and school **mentor** will assess the trainee's teaching skills. The ability to teach *Welsh as a second language* will be assessed using the 'Methodology Criteria' (**D**)[**CH** in the Welsh version]. The chart represents the 'ideal' to which all trainee teachers should aspire.

- To track their progress towards that ideal, and prepare them for future inspections, the Estyn inspection grades of 1-5 have been employed. The definitions attached to the grades are produced below:

1. VERY GOOD:	many good features, some exceptional
2. GOOD:	some good features and no major faults
3. SATISFACTORY:	good features outweighing some faults
4. UNSATISFACTORY:	a little satisfactory work but faults in important areas
5. POOR:	many faults

NAME: _____

SCHOOL: _____

PRESENTATION
- clear objectives – the context and what was to be achieved
- suitable vocabulary, patterns and phrases used
- suitable stimuli – visual, audio-visual and physical, etc.

EVERY DAY WELSH
- adapted to the learners' level (used e.g. to praise, greet, command, deal with different times of school day, etc.)
- ensured that the pupils understood
- some language used actively by the children

IMITATION, PRONUNCIATION AND INTONATION
- whole class/group/individual work
- used the printed word and singing/reading (in which natural repetition occured) as an aid

INTERDEPENDENCE OF LISTENING, ORAL, READING AND WRITTEN WORK
- displayed printed materials
- used computer programmes
- used reading material in which repetition occured naturally but which also sustained interest

ACTIVITIES (board games, dialogues, role-play, etc.)
- preparation
- sufficient opportunity to speak in a variety of activities
- class organisation

READ a story → **ORAL** work → **LISTENED TO** a sound tape → **WROTE** a word or two [L1], sentence and picture [12], various basic sentences [1,3,4]

EXTENDED PUPILS' GRASP OF LANGUAGE by:
- asking questions
- revising
- substituting
- encouraging language transfer

CONCLUSION
- opportunity provided for groups/pairs to perform –
- suitable feedback
- sufficient time allowed to revise
- noted what had been accomplished

VARIETY OF RESOURCES used to support the aims of the lesson

TEACHING exhibited
- careful observation and listening
- non–verbal and/or oral response
- interest and enjoyment

1	2	3	4	5

1. VERY GOOD
2. GOOD
3. SATISFACTORY
4. UNSATISFACTORY
5. POOR

WHY?
*   to celebrate success
*   to identify weaknesses
*   to plan future development

WHEN?
*   informally on a daily basis
*   formally on occasions
    Assessment conducted on a daily basis is called **formative assessment**.
    [The trainee teacher will decide how to proceed with the class/group or individuals on the basis of the feedback.]

    Assessment conducted at the end of a period is called **summative assessment**. It can take place at the end of a series of lessons, the end of a particular theme, or the end of a Key Stage.
    [It will be necessary to present a sufficient range of oral, reading and written tasks **over a period of time** before reaching any meaningful decisions regarding performance levels.]

THINGS TO CONSIDER
In **assessing from day to day**, does the trainee teacher:
*   ask questions to see whether the material has been understood?
    > e.g.   *Wyt ti'n hapus?*
    > *Beth sydd dan y ffenest?*
    > *Sut dywydd ydy hi heddiw?*
    > *Est ti i'r sinema neithiwr?*
*   display an ability to discover pupil difficulties?
    > e.g.   Can they differentiate between – *Mae **o** / Mae **hi. Mae** ceffyl …* / **Mae'r** *ceffyl …* ? Can they use the negative – '*dydy o ddim /dydy hi ddim*, etc.?
*   ask questions at the beginning of a new lesson/topic/theme, etc. to assess pupil capabilities?
    > e.g.   the patterns/phrases that can be transferred to the new lesson or theme
*   record the strengths (and weaknesses) revealed by the language activities – the listening, oral, reading and writing work?

During **summative assessments**, does the trainee teacher:
*   select a theme, specific aim or activity on which to base the assessment?
    > e.g.   THEME: hobbies .   AIM: Describe a place or person, express likes/dislikes.
    >
    > ACTIVITY:
    > play a board game (See: *Gêmau*)

*   select or devise a suitable assessment task?
*   display an ability to appropriately organise the class to undertake the task(s)?
    > e.g.   • pay attention to one discussion **group**
    > • listen to **individual** readers
    > • provide sufficient time for **individual** written tasks
    > • ensure that a tape-recorder/computer, etc, is available.
*   consider the extent to which the pupils are able to complete the task(s)?
*   use the information an assessment exercise provides to plan ahead and raise pupil standards?

- The following guidelines are intended as an aid for trainee teachers when assessing the language learning progress of their pupils. The levels to which they approximate are noted in brackets.

- KS1 pupils will be SATISFACTORY (i.e. will have reached Levels 1 or 2) when the FEATURES OF SATISFACTORY STANDARD describe their efforts more accurately than anything else.

- KS1 pupils will be GOOD (or will have reached Levels 2 or 3) when the FEATURES OF GOOD STANDARD describe their efforts more accurately than anything else.

KS1 ORAL (SPEAKING, LISTENING AND VIEWING)

FEATURES OF SATISFACTORY STANDARD (LEVELS 1/2)
Pupils able to
- passively comprehend within a range of contexts
- recall a range of words and patterns
- use short responses throughout KS1
- use a limited number of extended responses
- use correct but mechanical responses
- pronounce the majority of words and patterns clearly and accurately

Pupils:
- are diffident in adapting sentence patterns to more than one context
- possess an useful, though restricted, range of words, commands and sentence patterns

FEATURES OF GOOD STANDARD (LEVELS 2/3)
Pupils:
- make consistent progress in listening and comprehension
- have an understanding of vocabulary and patterns within a good range of topics
- understand the incidental language being used
- are able to ask and answer questions, greet, express opinions, feelings and needs
- can describe and explain within the confines of the language patterns learnt
- display enjoyment and enthusiasm

FEATURES OF SATISFACTORY STANDARD (LEVEL 3+)

Pupils:

- display a range of achievements: e.g. are able to command, ask and answer questions, take part in role-play,
- can compose a short simple speech about themselves and their interests
- show good comprehension of completed topics
- progress in understanding and oral proficiency throughout the KS
- exhibit continuity and progression throughout the KS

However:

- the range of vocabulary and patterns remains restricted
- pupils are diffident about using the language voluntarily – are reluctant to either comment or question of their own volition

FEATURES OF GOOD STANDARD (LEVEL 4+)

Pupils

- understand the oral contributions made by other pupils well
- can ask and answer a range of questions
- can produce descriptive comments with relative ease and accuracy
- can present information on an increasing range of subjects
- can respond effectively to each other during pair work
- can employ a variety of constructions, using the present and past tenses of the verb
- are increasingly able to talk in an extended manner throughout the KS.

FEATURES OF SATISFACTORY STANDARD (LEVELS 1/2)

Pupils able to:

- read such items as labels, captions and individual words
- respond satisfactorily to story-listening experiences
- read along with the teacher, displaying understanding, pleasure and an ability to volunteer oral contributions
- listen to a story on tape and follow it in print
- read print on a television and/or computer screen

FEATURES OF GOOD STANDARD (LEVELS 2/3)

Pupils able to:

- read suitable Welsh books independently
- enjoy browsing in a variety of texts
- read Welsh well enough to enjoy a story and the occasional factual text

FEATURES OF SATISFACTORY STANDARD (LEVELS 3+)

Pupils able to:

- read increasingly challenging whole texts, extracts or paragraphs throughout the KS
- read extracts aloud clearly and accurately
- exhibit an understanding of the content of the extracts when responding to questions on the text
- read personal work aloud with ease
- read worksheets

FEATURES OF GOOD STANDARD (LEVELS 4+)

Pupils able to:

- voluntarily read stories or reference material
- read appropriate, challenging texts meaningfully
- respond to reading material, being able to understand the ideas and the feelings presented in a text
- offer comment on the content of a text as well as respond to questions

FEATURES OF SATISFACTORY STANDARD (LEVELS 1/2)

Pupils able to:

- use Welsh in a range of suitable written tasks
- exhibit an understanding of the language in their written work
- complete tasks successfully
- exhibit a knowledge of written Welsh in their written work

FEATURES OF GOOD STANDARD (LEVELS 2/3)

Pupils able to:

- compose freely, to denote preference or need, or write a short descriptive or factual account

FEATURES OF SATISFACTORY STANDARD (LEVELS 3+)

Pupils able to:

- complete a suitable range of written tasks, answer questions, present information and complete dialogues
- exhibit an understanding of the work in hand in their written work
- compose simple texts, using a string of sentences and varying the use of language patterns to some degree
- show progress throughout the KS

FEATURES OF GOOD STANDARD (LEVELS 4+)

Pupils able to:

- complete written tasks confidently and independently
- display a good measure of accuracy (in spelling, verb forms and construction) in free composition
- use a sequence of sentences and a range of vocabulary and language patterns in free composition
- complete extended work which presents a challenge and reflects progress year on year

EXAMPLES OF THE KIND OF ACTIVITIES AND LANGUAGE TASKS WHICH CAN BE USED TO ASSESS AND RECORD PROGRESS

ORACY

- listening to audio-visual stimuli
- suitably responding to audio-visual stimuli or the teacher
- role-playing
- conversing/discussing
- expressing an opinion simply
- presenting and receiving information
- conveying personal and imagined feelings and experiences
- discussing reading materials using such key words as: *awdur, plot, disgrifiadau,* etc.

READING

- reading aloud
- reading independently
- using reference books
- reading excerpts of a story to others

WRITING

- writing an account to accompany a series of pictures
- writing short accounts e.g. a note, letter, etc.
- writing stories
- presenting information
- expressing an opinion
- making appropriate use of dictionaries and word lists.

(see also page 123)

- There follows a list of 'useful assessment statements … ' which may be of use to the trainee teacher when beginning to assess the LISTENING/ORAL progress of pupils

LISTENING/UNDERSTANDING
- can understand individual words/clauses/simple sentences
- can understand the content of material using more difficult patterns and vocabulary

COMMUNICATION/ORACY
General
Able to:
- use '*Cymraeg Pob Dydd*' e.g. greet, thank, etc.
- pronounce and intone comprehensibly
- pronounce and intone clearly and with ease
- respond in a cryptic and limited manner
- respond showing some willingness to elaborate
- show initiative i.e. to give more language back than was received

Specific
Able to:
- ask and answer the most familiar questions
- ask and answer general questions
- ask and answer a wide range of questions★
- describe experiences in simple terms
- describe experiences effectively and interestingly★
- describe an event/place/building/person (a) superficially (b) adequately (c) fully and in an engaging manner★
- present and search for information
- re-present short pieces of simple information
- re-present basic information
- give simple instructions
- give detailed instructions★
- express an opinion giving reasons★
  ★A pupil will reach these objectives at Level 4 and above.

LANGUAGE RESOURCES
Pupils able to:
- spell simple words correctly
- spell most common words correctly
- use a limited vocabulary
- use an adequate vocabulary
- use simple affirmative/interrogative/negative sentences
- exhibit an awareness of form
- use affirmative and negative responses to questions ('Yes' and 'No')

a)	accurately on occasion
b)	in a consistently accurate manner

- use prepositions

a)	accurately on occasion
b)	in a consistently accurate manner

- use tenses of the verb

a)	accurately on occasion
b)	in a consistently accurate manner

Part 3
Appendix

EXAMPLES OF LANGUAGE LEARNING ACTIVITIES AND PUPIL WORK

REFERENCE TO UNIT		Pages
5.	**Pair work**	90-98
	• Describing and enquiring about an event	
	• *'Ti a Fi'* – assorted games, WJEC	
	• *'Dwy gegin'* -' information gap' activity	
	• *'Sawl?'* – counting; using prepositions	
	• *'Cerdded i'r ysgol'* – another 'information gap' activity	
	• ★Pair work – *Ffeindio Partner:* 'Finding a Partner' (See 19 below)	
	Questionnaire work:	99-101
	Examples of simple questionnaire and pair work · : Gweld	
	: Teimlo	
	• Framework for **creating** a **dialogue**	
14.	**Everyday Welsh**	102-107
	• An example of a lesson presenting *'Iaith Pob Dydd'* on levels 1/2	
	• **Helpwr Heddiw** (Today's Helper):	
	from *'Siarad Cymraeg yn y Dosbarth'* Non ap Emlyn pp.28-31	
16.	**Cross-curricular teaching/learning**	108-110
	• Worksheet depicting opportunities for cross-curricular work	
	• An example of cross-curricular work – *'Y Normaniaid'*	
17.	**Using video resources**	111-112
	• Mr. Bean worksheet	
19.	**Reading**	113-121
	• Examples of books suitable for KS1/KS2	
	• Examples of reading and revision records	
	• Reading and writing stemming from an activity such as a class game –	
	'Pa offer wyt ti angen?'★ (See 5 above)	
	• One way of using a story	
20.	**Writing**	122-137
	• Raising writing standards	
	• Examples of different kinds of writing on levels 1-6	
21.	**Role-play**	138-145
	• The kind of considerations teachers have in mind when writing a script	A
	• An example of 'developing language' on levels 1/2	B
	• An example of 'developing language' on level 2	C
	• An example of basing a task on role-play	D (CH)
	• Role-play using simple information gaps	E (D)
	• An example of role-play based on flash cards	F/G (DD/E)
22.	**Games**	146-153
	• Class games – level 5	
	• Board game – *'Ble mae Paris?'* – question and answer cards	
	• Computer programmes and useful Compact Discs	

GWAITH PÂR: DISGRIFIO A HOLI AM DDIGWYDDIAD
PAIR WORK: DESCRIBING AND ENQUIRING ABOUT AN EVENT

I ddechrau, bydd Partner 1 yn holi Partner 2 am ei (g)wyliau gan ddefnyddio'r 'prociadau cof' *(prompts)* sydd ar y cardiau. Yna bydd Partner 2 yn holi Partner 1. Bydd Partner 1 yn adrodd yn ôl ar wyliau Partner 2 ac i'r gwrthwyneb.

Partner 1 will ask Partner 2 about his/her holiday using the prompts on his/her card. Then Partner 2 will repeat the process with Partner 1. Partner 1 will then report back on Partner 2's holiday and vice-versa.

- *Ble est ti/aethoch chi am wyliau?*   - *Sut oedd y tywydd?*

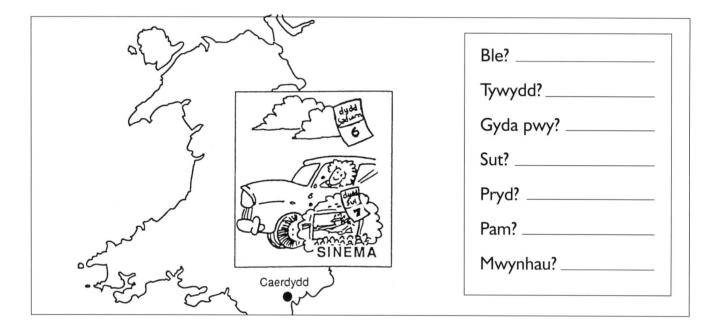

Gêm 1. Rhannau'r Corff.

Symudwch ar hyd y trac trwy daflu'r dis.
Pan dych chi'n glanio ar y sgwâr siâp mae'n rhaid i chi enwi'r rhan o'r corff yn y llun.

Gêm 3. Dillad.

Symudwch ar hyd y trac trwy daflu'r dis.
Pan dych chi'n glanio ar y sgwâr siâp mae'n rhaid enwi'r dillad mae pobl yn wisgo ar y rhan o'r corff.

Gêm 4. Teimladau.

Mae bob llun ar y bwrdd yn dangos teimlad.
Symudwch ar hyd y trac trwy daflu'r dis. Pan dych chi'n glanio ar y sgwâr siâp mae'n rhaid i chi ddweud:

Dw i'n teimlo'n ...

neu

Mae e/hi'n teimlo'n ...

Set Glas - Dillad

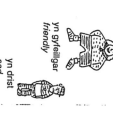

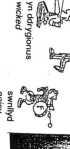

crys T	T shirt	
siaced	jacket	
het	hat	
siwmper	jumper	
esgidiau	shoes	
sbectol	spectacles	
sanau	socks	
trowsus	trousers	
sgert	skirt	
menig	gloves	
sgarff	scarf	
tei	tie	

Game 3. Clothes.

Move along the track after throwing the die.
When you land on a body shape then you must name items of clothing worn on one or two of parts of the body highlighted.

Gêm 3. Estynlad.

Symudwch ar hyd y trac trwy daflu'r dis fel Gêm 3. Pan dych chi'n glanio ar y sgwariau oren mae'n rhaid i chi godi cerdyn ac enwi'r dilledyn ar y cerdyn.

Game 3. Extended.

Using the Clothes Cards play the game as game 3 but in addition if you land on an orange square then you must pick up a card and name the item of clothing on the card.
If you answer correctly then you may move forward.
If you answer incorrectly then you must miss a turn.

Game 4. Emotions.

The figures on the game display different emotions.
These are the emotions displayed from start to finish.
The game is played as before but when you land on a body shape you must say how the person feels.

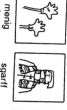

yn gyfeillgar	friendly
yn drist	sad
yn gas	nasty
yn ofnus	frightened
yn dost	ill
yn flinedig	tired
yn ddrygionus	wicked
yn dawel	quiet
swnllyd	noisy

---

body highlighted in that particular body shape.
If you cannot answer then you must miss a turn.
The first to finish wins the game.

Gêm 1. Estynlad.

Symudwch ar hyd y trac trwy daflu'r dis. Pan dych chi'n glanio ar y sgwâr siâp mae'n rhaid enwi'r rhannau o'r corff yn y sgwâr.
Hefyd os dych chi'n glanio ar un o'r sgwariau oren mae'n rhaid i chi godi cerdyn ac enwi'r rhan o'r corff.

Set Gwyrdd - Rhannau'r Corff

bol/bola	tummy
pen	head
braich	arm
troed	foot
llaw	hand
wyneb	face
coes	leg
gwddf	neck
clust	ear
ysgwydd	shoulder
pen-glin	knee
gwallt	hair

Game 1. Parts of the body.

Os dych chi'n gywir, symudwch ymlaen.
Os na, rhaid i chi golli tro.

Game 1. Extended.

Play the game as above, bringing the orange squares on the board and additional Parts of the Body Cards (Rhannau'r Corff) into play.
If you land on an orange square then you must pick up a card and name the body part.
If you answer correctly then you may move forward.
If you answer incorrectly then you must miss a turn.

Gêm 2. Salwch.

Symudwch ar hyd y trac trwy daflu'r dis.
Pan dych chi'n glanio ar y sgwâr siâp mae'n rhaid i chi ddewis un, dwy, tair rhan o'r corff a dweud:

"Mae ... tost da fi"
"Mae ...tost ganddo fe/ganddi hi."

neu

"Mae gen i ...tost"
"Mae ganddo/ganddi ... tost."

Game 2. Illness.

Move along the track, after throwing the die.
When you land on a body shape then you must choose one, two or three parts of the body and say:

Mae ...tost da fe/da hi.
He/She has ...
Mae gen i ...tost.
I have ...
Mae ganddo/ganddi ...tost
He/She has ...

or

Mae ...tost da fi.
I have ...

If you answer correctly then you may move forward.
If you answer incorrectly then you must miss a turn.

MAE GANDDO FOLA TOST.

91

Gêm 5. Disgrifiadau

Symudwch ar hyd y trac trwy daflu'r dis. Pan ydych chi'n glanio ar y *sgwâr siâp* mae'n rhaid i chi godi cerdyn o'r blwch cardiau sy'n dal y Cardiau Disgrifio a disgrifio'r person.

Game 5. Descriptions

Move along the track after throwing the dice. When you land on the body shape you must take a card from the card box which holds the Description Cards and describe the person.

Gêm 5 Estyniad

Symudwch ar hyd y trac trwy daflu'r dis. Pan ydych chi'n glanio ar y *sgwariau oren* mae'n rhaid i chi godi Cerdyn Disgrifio a disgrifio'r person.

Game 5. Extension

Play the game as usual.
If you land on an orange square you must pick up a Description Card and describe the person.

| yn fyr | yn dal | yn denau | yn dew |
| *short* | *tall* | *thin* | *fat* |

| yn fawr | yn fach | yn gryf | yn wan | yn ifanc | yn hen | yn foel | yn flewog |
| *big* | *small* | *strong* | *weak* | *young* | *old* | *bald* | *hairy* |

DWY GEGIN TWO KITCHENS:	LEVEL 3

AIM:	• Learn to count; question and answer; use prepositions accurately

PURPOSE OF GAME	• Discover who has the greater number of kitchen utensils/spiders • Enable the pupils to question one another

LANGUAGE:	• *Sawl [★cwpan] sydd yna?* • *Sawl [cwpan] sydd (gy)da/gen ti?* • Numbers 1–20 and kitchen furniture and equipment: *★tebot sosban, fforc, cyllell, llwy, cwpan, soser, gwydryn, plât, powlen (dysgl), pry cop/corryn,* will be used. ★ denotes the language items that will be exchanged.

HOW TO PLAY:	• Divide class into pairs • Hand out copies of picture 'A' to a member of each pair • Distribute copies of picture 'B' to the rest • 'A's task is to discover (by asking questions) how many things 'B' has in his/her kitchen and vice-versa. For example: *Sawl [cwpan] sydd (gy)da/gen ti?* *Sawl [plât] sydd (gy)da/gen ti*

AT OTHER TIMES (Level 4) the plural forms may be used instead:

> *Faint o [gwpanau] sydd (gy)da/gen ti?*
> *Faint o [blatiau] sydd (gy)da/gen ti?*

(Gemau Cyfathrebol Harrap: J. Hadfield. Addasiad D. Hughes Pritchard)

Partner 1	Holwch eich partner a rhowch gylch o gwmpas yr atebion cywir.
	Ask your partner the following questions and circle the correct answers.

Ydy Ann yn croesi'r bont?	Ydy	Nac ydy	
Ydy Huw yn pasio'r garej?	Ydy	Nac ydy	
Sawl bachgen sy'n pasio'r siop?	Un	Dau	Tri
Sawl merch sy'n pasio'r siop?	Un	Dau	Tri
Ydy John yn cerdded y llwybr?	Ydy	Nac ydy	
Oes merch yn cerdded y llwybr?	Oes	Nac oes	
Oes dau fachgen yn pasio'r garej?	Oes	Nac oes	
Sawl plentyn sy'n croesi'r nant?	Dim un	Un	Dau
Sawl merch sy'n pasio'r garej?	Dim un	Un / Dwy	Tair
Oes dwy ferch yn pasio'r garej?	Oes	Nac oes	

Partner 2	Edrychwch ar y map ac atebwch gwestiynau eich partner.
	Study the map and answer your partner's questions.

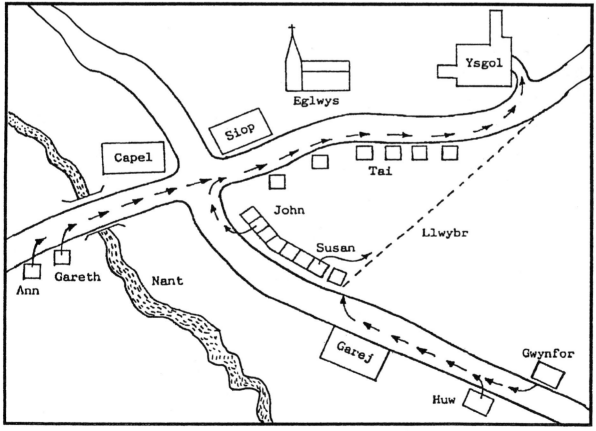

(Bydd ambell bâr yn perfformio i'r dosbarth ar ddiwedd y gweithgaredd.
Some pairs will perform for the class at the end of the activity).

Sut i chwarae/How to play

- *Rhoi'r disgyblion mewn parau.*
  The pupils pair.

- *Gofyn i un o bob pâr sefyll (Disgybl 1) ac un eistedd (Disgybl 2).*
  One member of each pair stands (Pupil 1), the other sits (Pupil 2).

- *Rhoi copi o 'Gêm Ffeindio Partner: A' (tudalen 97) i bob Disgybl 1 a chopi o 'Ffeindio Partner: B'*
  (tudalen 98) i bob Disgybl 2
  'Ffeindio Partner: A' (page 97) is distributed to all Pupil 1's and
  'Ffeindio Partner: B' (page 98) to all Pupils 2's.

- *Ymarfer y ddeialog sy'n dilyn:*
  The following dialogue is then practised:

Disgybl 1:	*Pa offer wyt ti eisiau (isio/isie)?*
Pupil 1:	What equipment do you want?
Disgybl 2:	*Dw i eisiau tywel a gogls, os gwelwch yn dda.*
Pupil 2:	I want a towel and some goggles, please.
Disgybl 1:	*Dyma ti (rhoi'r cerdyn sy'n dangos tywel a gogls i Disgybl 2).*
Pupil 1:	Here you are (gives the card depicting a towel and goggles to Pupil 2).

- *Os nad oes gan Disgybl 1 yr offer iawn bydd yn dweud:*
  If Pupil 1 does not have the correct equipment he/she will say:

Disgybl 1:	*Pa offer wyt ti eisiau?*
Pupil 1:	What equipment do you want?
Disgybl 2:	*Dw i eisiau tywel a gogls, os gwelwch yn dda.*
Pupil 2:	I want a towel and some goggles, please.
Disgybl 1:	*Mae'n ddrwg gen i, does gen i ddim tywel a gogls.*
Pupil 1:	I'm sorry, I haven't got a towel and goggles.

Ar ôl i Ddisgybl 1 ymateb naill ai'n gadarnhaol neu'n negyddol, tro Disgybl 2 yw cychwyn ar yr un ddeialog. Ar ôl peth amser gall y rhai sy'n eistedd newid lle â'r rhai sy'n sefyll.
After Pupil 1 has answered either in the affirmative or negative, it will be Pupil 2's turn to start the dialogue. After a while those pupils sitting down can change places with those standing.

Yn dilyn y gwaith llafar gellir defnyddio'r daflen 'Pa offer wyt ti angen?' i wneud gwaith ysgrifennu (Gweler 'Gêmau' t. 150/151).
As a follow up to the oral work the pupils can be invited to undertake written work using the worksheet entitled '*Pa offer wyt ti angen?*' (See: *Gêmau pp. 150/151*).

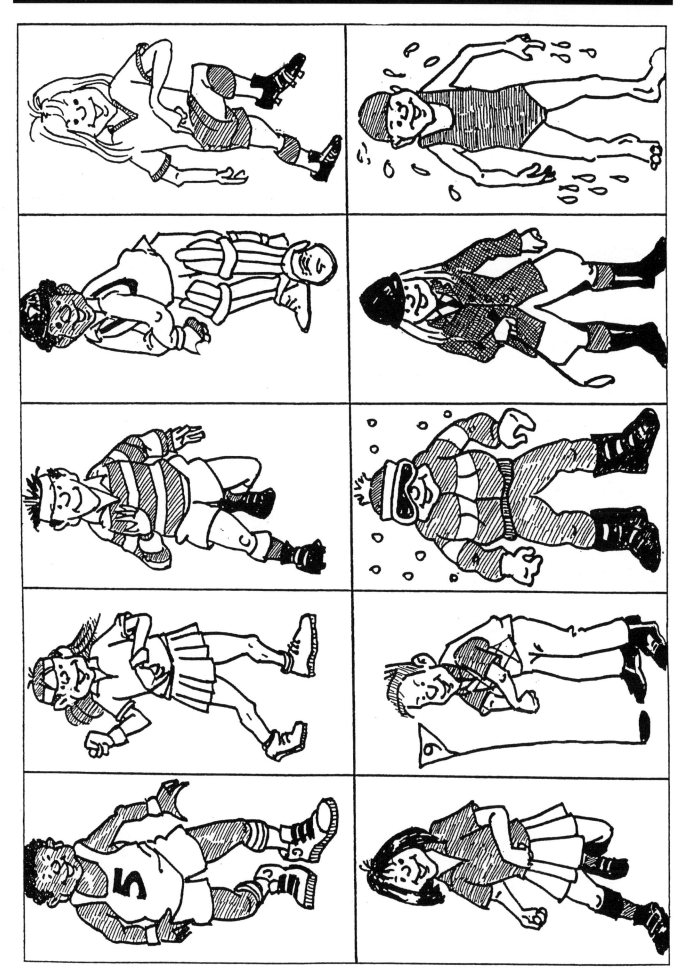

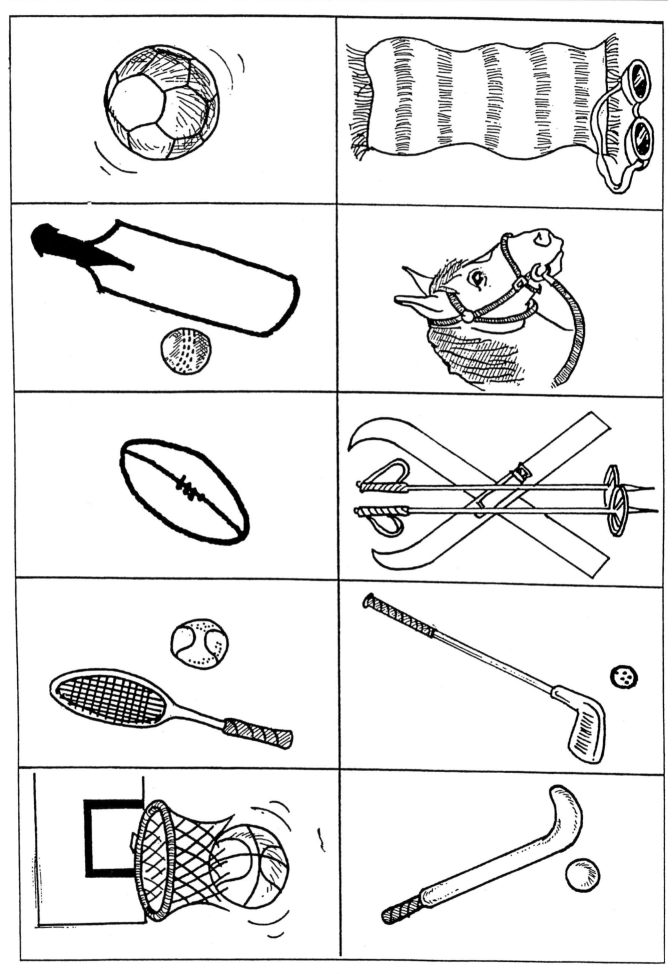

• *DYDDIAD* : DATE _____

Gweld

Gogledd/North	*De*/South
Beth ddaru ti weld? *Ddaru mi weld …*	*Beth wnest ti weld?* *Fe wnes i weld …* *Beth welaist ti?* *Fe welais i …*

1. *Mae deg peth ar y tray*
2. *Edrych ar y pethau am ddau funud*
   (*Y darpar athro/awes yn rhoi lliain dros y pethau*)
3. *Gofyn i dy ffrind – Beth ddaru ti weld/Beth welaist ti?*
4. *Rho* ✓ *yn y bocs os ydy o/e/hi wedi gweld y peth*
5. *Rho* ✗ *yn y bocs os dydy o/e/hi ddim wedi gweld y peth*

There are ten things on the tray
Look at them for two minutes
(Trainee teacher covers the tray)
Ask your friend – What did you see?
Place a ✓ in the box if he/she has seen the object
Place a ✗ in the box if he/she has not seen the object

Rwber		Pren Mesur	
Pensil		Afal	
Cwpan		Siswrn	
Blodyn		Fferins	
Pen		Sialc	
Glud		Tâp selo	
Papur		Llyfr	
Fideo		Câs pensil	

DYDDIAD : DATE _____

Teimlo

Bag Teimlo

1. *Mae 10 peth yn y bag*
   There are 10 things in the bag

2. *Gofyn i dy ffrind deimlo rhywbeth yn y bag*
   Ask your friend to feel for an object in the bag

3. *Gofyn i dy ffrind*
   Ask your friend

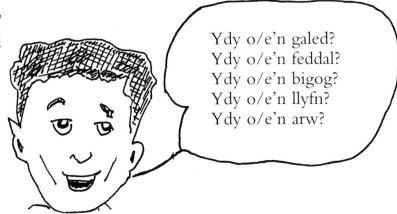

Ydy o/e'n galed?
Ydy o/e'n feddal?
Ydy o/e'n bigog?
Ydy o/e'n llyfn?
Ydy o/e'n arw?

4. *Os ydy e/o/hi'n ateb 'Ydy' – rho ✔ yn y bocs.*
   If he/she answers 'Yes' place a ✔ in the box

5. *Os ydy e/o/hi'n ateb 'Nac ydy' – rho ✗ yn y bocs*
   If he/she answers 'No' place an ✗ in the box.

Enw	galed	feddal	bigog	llyfn	arw	Beth ydy o/e?

• Greet	*Cyfarch*
• The weather	*Y tywydd*
• Offer help	*Cynnig help*
• Ask for something	*Gofyn am rywbeth*
• Ask what size/colour	*Gofyn pa liw/maint*
• Answer giving details	*Ateb gyda manylion lliw/maint,* etc.
• Anything else?	*Rhywbeth arall?*
• Choose something	*Dewis rhywbeth*
• Is that everything?	*Y cwbl?*
• Ask the price	*Faint?*
• Give price	*Rhoi'r pris*
• Say farewell	*Ffarwelio*

When teaching *Cymraeg Pob Dydd* (Everyday Welsh) the trainee teacher will:

GREET   Get the pupils to imitate and use greetings effectively

RESPOND   Teach pupils how to respond positively in a variety of ways e.g.
Iawn, diolch/Da iawn, diolch. Go lew/gweddol. Wedi blino, etc.

COMMAND   Model and teach classroom instructions ensuring that the pupils understand them. He/she will also motivate the pupils to command, give instructions, organise, perform/make things to given instructions, etc.

Eisteddwch	*Grŵp coch*
Dim siarad	*Caewch y drws*
Da iawn	*Dewch yma*
Dos/Cer i nôl …	*Ewch i nôl …*
Grŵp glas	

ENQUIRE   Ensure that the pupils are able to ask questions in Welsh e.g. '*Beth ydy [terrible] yn Gymraeg?*' *Ga i [rwber] Miss? Sut ydych chi'n … ?* etc.

USE DAILY RITUALS   Teach the pupils
(i)   how to respond during registration, for example *Yma/Ddim yma*.
(ii)   Other relevant responses e.g. *Mae hi/o/e'n sâl/hwyr/yn y toiled …* will also be introduced and practised.

A registration role-play session can be set up or dialogues similar to the following practised:

Fersiwn y Gogledd (Northen Version)

Athrawes:	A rwan – y gofrestr. John Blackwell?
John:	Yma, Miss.
Athrawes:	Annette Price?
Simon:	Yma, Miss.
Athrawes:	Stephen Davies? … Stephen Davies? – ddim yma? Ble mae Stephen Davies?
Plentyn:	Mae o'n sâl.
Athrawes:	Diolch Siân. Kevin Edwards?
Kevin:	Yma, Miss.
Athrawes:	Rhys Griffiths? … Rhys Griffiths? Ble mae Rhys Griffiths?
Plentyn:	Yn y toiled, Miss.
Athrawes:	Iawn. William Jones? Ble mae William Jones?
Plentyn:	Mae o yn y toiled hefyd, Miss.
Athrawes:	Kevin – dos i nôl Rhys a William.
Kevin:	Iawn, Miss.

When teaching *Cymraeg Pob Dydd* (Everyday Welsh) the trainee teacher will:

GREET   Get the pupils to imitate and use greetings effectively.

RESPOND   Teach pupils how to respond positively in a variety of ways e.g.
                           Iawn, diolch/Da iawn, diolch. Go lew/gweddol. Wedi blino, etc.

COMMAND   Model and teach classroom instructions ensuring that the pupils understand
                           them. He/she will also motivate the pupils to command, give instructions,
                           organise, perform/make things to given instructions, etc.

Eisteddwch	*Grŵp coch*
Dim siarad	*Caewch y drws*
Da iawn	*Dewch yma*
Dos/Cer i nôl …	*Ewch i nôl …*
Grŵp glas	

ENQUIRE   Ensure that the pupils are able to ask questions in Welsh e.g. *Beth ydy [terrible]
                           yn Gymraeg? Ga i [rwber] Miss? Sut ydych chi'n …* ? etc.

USE DAILY   Teach the pupils
                           (i)   how to respond during registration, for example *Yma/Ddim yma*.
RITUALS   (ii) Other relevant responses e.g. *Mae hi/o/e'n sâl/hwyr/yn y toiled …* will
                                 also be introduced and practised.

                           A registration role-play session can be set up or dialogues similar to the
                           following practised:

Fersiwn y De (Southern Version)

Athrawes:	A nawr – y gofrestr. John Blackwell?
John:	Yma, Miss.
Athrawes:	Annette Price?
Simon:	Yma, Miss.
Athrawes:	Stephen Davies? … Stephen Davies? – ddim yma? Ble mae Stephen Davies?
Plentyn:	Mae e'n dost.
Athrawes:	Diolch Siân. Kevin Edwards?
Kevin:	Yma, Miss.
Athrawes:	Rhys Griffiths? … Rhys Griffiths? Ble mae Rhys Griffiths?
Plentyn:	Yn y tŷ bach, Miss.
Athrawes:	Iawn. William Jones? Ble mae William Jones?
Plentyn:	Mae e yn y tŷ bach hefyd, Miss.
Athrawes:	Kevin – dos/cer i nôl Rhys a William.
Kevin:	Iawn, Miss.

One effective way of using Welsh in the classroom is to appoint a *Helpwr Heddiw/*Today's Helper, to assist in the various procedures associated with the school day.

This unit includes various examples of the role of the *Helpwr Heddiw.* His/her contribution is included in bold type in order to illustrate the language patterns/vocabulary being used.

- **AMSER COFRESTRU/REGISTRATION**

Athrawes:	Bore da, blant.
Plant:	Bore da, Mrs Jones.
Athrawes:	Pwy ydy *Helpwr Heddiw?*
Simon:	**Fi, Miss.**
Athrawes:	Iawn, eisteddwch blant. Simon, tyrd yma … Y Gofrestr.
H. H.:	**John Blackwell, wyt ti yma?**
John:	Yma.
H.H.:	**Yma.**
Athrawes:	Iawn.
H.H.:	**John Crawford, wyt ti yma?**
John:	Yma.
H.H.:	**Yma. Stephen Davies, wyt ti yma? …**
	Stephen Davies, wyt ti yma? … Ddim yma.
Athrawes:	Ble mae Stephen Davies?
Lisa:	Mae o efo'r Pennaeth.
Athrawes:	Diolch Lisa. Iawn, Simon …
H.H.:	**Mark Edwards, wyt ti yma … ?**

> **Wyt ti yma? –** *Are you here?*
> **Yma –** *Here*
> **Dim yma/Ddim yma –** *Not Here*

- **AMSER CINIO/LUNCH TIME**

Athrawes:	*Helpwr Heddiw,* tyrd yma – Mae hi'n amser cinio.
H.H.:	**Tacluswch eich byrddau! ... Dim siarad! ... Sefwch! ... Dwylo efo'i gilydd! ... caewch eich llygaid!**
Pawb:	'Diolch i Ti am ein bwyd bob dydd. Amen'.
H.H.:	**Bwrdd glas, cerddwch allan yn araf ... Bwrdd coch, cerddwch allan yn araf ... Bwrdd melyn, cerddwch allan yn araf ... Bwrdd gwyrdd, cerddwch allan yn araf ... Bwrdd oren, cerddwch allan yn araf.**
Athrawes:	Diolch, Simon.

> **Tacluswch eich byrddau!** Tidy your tables
> **Dwylo efo'i gilydd!** Hands together!
> **Caewch eich llygaid!** Close your eyes!

- **AMSER MYND ADRE/TIME TO GO HOME**

Athrawes:	Amser mynd adre – *Helpwr Heddiw,* tyrd yma.
H.H.:	**Tacluswch! ... Dim siarad.**
Athrawes:	Dwedwch 'Diolch' wrth *Helpwr Heddiw* – Simon.
Plant:	Diolch.
Athrawes:	Rwan – pwy ydy *Helpwr Yfory?* – Eleri! Iawn!

> **Dwedwch 'Diolch' wrth Helpwr Heddiw**
> *Thank Helpwr Heddiw*
> Helpwr Yfory – *Tomorrow's Helper*

Even the youngest children can play the part of **Helpwr Heddiw** – and enjoy doing so. The following are examples of the assistance given by the **Helpwr Heddiw** in an infants' class. They were not scripted or rehearsed for the tape.

- **AMSER COFRESTRU/REGISTRATION TIME**

(The names of the children have been clearly written on a card for the *Helpwr Heddiw,* who reads it while the teacher marks the register).

Mrs Nichol:	*Helpwr Heddiw,* tyrd i eistedd i lawr.
H.H.:	**Ydy Gemma yma?**
Gemma:	Prynhawn da James a Mrs Nichol.
H.H.:	**Sut wyt ti heddiw?**
Gemma:	Da iawn diolch.
H.H.:	**Ydy Dafydd yma?**
Pawb:	Dydy Dafydd ddim yma.
Mrs Nichol:	Ble mae Dafydd?
Pawb:	Sâl. O biti.
H.H.:	**Ydy Marie yma?**
Marie:	Prynhawn da James a Mrs Nichol.
H.H.:	**Sut wyt ti heddiw?**
Marie:	Da iawn, diolch. Sut wyt ti James – a Mrs Nichol?
H.H.:	**Hapus.**
Mrs Nichol:	Hapus, diolch.
H.H.:	**Ydy Jacinta yma?**
Jacinta:	Prynhawn da, bawb. Sut wyt ti (Mrs Nichol)?
Mrs Nichol:	Hapus iawn, diolch. Iawn, eistedd i lawr *Helpwr Heddiw.* Diolch.

> Ydy ... yma? *Is ... here?*
> Ydy – *Yes*
> Nac ydy/Nag ydy – *No*
> Dydy ... ddim yma – *... isn't here*
> O biti! O bechod! – *What a pity!*

- **AMSER SNAC/SNACK TIME**

Athrawes:	Iawn, mae'n amser snac. *Helpwr Heddiw*, wyt ti'n barod?
H.H.:	**Ydw ... Pwy biau'r bisged?**
Plentyn:	Fi – diolch, *Helpwr Heddiw*.
H.H,:	**Pwy biau'r afal?**
Plentyn:	Fi, diolch yn fawr, *Helpwr Heddiw*
H.H.:	**Pwy biau'r ddiod?**
Plentyn:	Diolch yn fawr, *Helpwr Heddiw*.
H.H.:	**Pwy biau'r banana?**
Plentyn:	Fi. Diolch, *Helpwr Heddiw*.
Athrawes:	Da iawn, *Helpwr Heddiw*. Diolch yn fawr. Eistedd i lawr.

Pwy biau ... ? *Whose is ... ?*
Pwy biau'r ... ? *Whose is the ... ?*

Pwy biau'r afal? *Whose is the apple?*
Pwy biau'r bisged? *Whose is the biscuit?*
Pwy biau'r pop? *Whose is the pop?*
Pwy biau'r ddiod? *Whose is the drink?*

Wyt ti'n barod? – *Are you ready?*

- **AMSER CHWARAE/PLAY TIME**

Athrawes:	Iawn, amser chwarae bawb. Hanna, iawn?
H.H.:	**Ydw.**
Plentyn:	Ga i fynd allan os gwelwch yn dda?
H.H.:	**Cei.**
Plentyn:	Ga i fynd allan os gwelwch yn dda?
H.H.:	**Cei.**
Plentyn:	Ga i fynd allan os gwelwch yn dda?
H.H.:	**Cei.**
Plentyn:	Ga i fynd allan os gwelwch yn dda?
H.H.:	**Cei.**
Athrawes	*Helpwr Heddiw,* gofyn i fi.
H.H.:	**Ga i fynd allan os gwelwch yn dda?**
Athrawes:	Na chei ... Cei, siŵr. Cer allan.

Helpwr Heddiw also assists when the children are dismissed for lunch:

Grŵp coch – Ewch i'r toiled i olchi dwylo.
Grŵp glas – Ewch i'r toiled i olchi dwylo.
Grŵp melyn – Ewch i'r toiled i olchi dwylo, etc.

Golchi dwylo – *to wash (your) hands*

(The main purpose of this chart is to highlight the cross-curricular opportunities offered by different 'subjects' to the language teacher)

WELSH	SCIENCE	MATHEMATICS
Create: stories, descriptions, reviews, invitations. Write: poetry, cards, postcards, diaries, scripts, posters, captions, labels, advertisements, reports, newspapers, questionnaires, etc.	Plan experiments, give instructions/directions, forecast results, offer comments e.g. on graphs, tables, results, etc.	Number work, money work, name shapes, measure, give approximations, use questionnaires, mental arithmetic, etc.
RELIGIOUS EDUCATION Re-tell stories, compose prayers, rules, hymns. Label, describe traditions, ceremonies, etc.	**CROSS-CURRICULAR OPPORTUNITIES** Oracy, Reading and Writing	INFORMATION and COMMUNICATIONS TECHNOLOGY Co-write and edit on a computer, collect/collate/ interpret data, play language games, word processing, etc.
GEOGRAPHY Interview, use questionnaires, describe, plan, create signs, use symbols, make maps, provide directions, etc.		DESIGN and TECHNOLOGY Plan/design, label diagrams, describe, create lists/menus/ advertisements/posters, etc.
PHYSICAL EDUCATION Create rules, give directions, plan, report, use questionnaires, record results, etc.	MUSIC, ART, DRAMA Listen to and/or create songs, respond to poetry and music, explain and evaluate art processes, advertise. Use slogans, captions, scripts. Provide or follow directions. Characterise, create posters, etc.	HISTORY Search for information, describe, interview, persuade, empathise, etc.

1. Deall, drilio a dysgu. *Understand, drill and learn*

MAE GANDDO FO	helmed		**MAE GANDDI HI**	ffrog	hir
He's got a	gleddyf		*She's got a*	glogyn	cynnes
	arfbais			felt	cryf
	bicell			blethi	mawr
	darian			lewys	

DOES GANDDO FO DDIM	het		**DOES GANDDI HI DDIM**	cap
He hasn't got a	ambarél		*She hasn't got a*	sgert
	siwmper			trowsus
	tei			bag

2. Holi ac Ateb *Question and Answer*

Has he/she got a?   Oes ganddo fo helmed/ambarél/glogyn?

Oes ganddi hi blethi/sgert/bicell?

Oes, mae ganddo fo …

Nac oes, does ganddi hi ddim …

Plentyn yn dod i flaen y dosbarth, yn pwyntio at wrthrych yn y lluniau, ac yn gofyn cwestiwn wedi ei seilio ar y patrwm uchod. Y sawl sy'n ateb yn gywir yn cymryd ei le/lle. *Child goes to the front of the class, points at an object in the pictures, and asks a question based on the above pattern. The child who answers correctly takes his/her place.*

1. **Deall, drilio a dysgu.** *Understand, drill and learn*

MAE *He's got a*	helmed cleddyf afrbais picell tarian	**GYDA FE**	**MAE** *She's got a*	ffrog clogyn belt plethi llewys	hir cynnes cryf mawr	**GYDA HI**
DOES DIM *He hasn't got a*	het ambarél siwmper tei	**GYDA FE**	**DOES DIM** *She hasn't got a*	cap sgert trowsus bag		**GYDA HI**

2. **Holi ac Ateb**   *Question and Answer*
Has he/she got a?

Oes helmed/ambarél/clogyn (gy)da fe?
Oes plethi/sgert/picell (gy)da hi?
Oes, mae … (gy)da fe.
Nac oes, does dim … (gy)da hi/fe.

Plentyn yn dod i flaen y dosbarth, yn pwyntio at wrthrych yn y lluniau, ac yn gofyn cwestiwn wedi ei seilio ar y patrwm uchod. Y sawl sy'n ateb yn gywir yn cymryd ei le/lle. *Child goes to the front of the class, points at an object in the pictures, and asks a question based on the above pattern. The child who answers correctly takes his/her place.*

DEFNYDDIO ADNODDAU FIDEO / USING VIDEO RESOURCES

STEP 1   Use pre-viewing activities whenever appropriate. Play and watch the video clip. Emphasise that it is not necessary for the viewer to understand every single word. Set specific viewing tasks for older pupils.

STEP 2   More detailed teaching. Draw attention to a word or pattern, before re-viewing the clip. Pause the tape, to highlight the aspects of language being taught or to allow time to undertake activities based on the clip.

STEP 3   Reinforce **STEP 2** by replaying the clip, this time without stopping. If the material is challenging, the tape may be stopped, in appropriate places, to provide further opportunities for language 'intake'.

ENGHREIFFTIAU O WEITHGAREDDAU FIDEO / EXAMPLES OF VIDEO ACTIVITIES

The activities which follow (based on 'A Visit to the Dentist' from the video 'The Trouble with Mr. Bean') are taken from the volume *Llunyddiaeth*, Geraint Wyn Jones (1995), CAI, Llangefni, pages 16, 17, and 18.

For KS2 Levels 2/3

(i)   View the following clip. You may make notes, if you wish, during the viewing. These will help you later to recall the story in sequence.

(i)   Find a partner.

(ii)   Tell the story, working with your partner.

(iii)   Report back to the class and compare and contrast the various versions.

For Levels 4/5 and higher

(i)   View the following clip carefully. You will then be required to answer detailed questions.

     Any tense or person etc. can be practised when formulating such questions, e.g.:

1.   *Sawl bin sbwriel mae Mr. Bean yn eu taro efo/gyda'r car?*
     Sawl bin sbwriel wnaeth Mr. Bean eu taro efo/gyda'r car?
     Sawl bin sbwriel ddaru Mr. Bean eu taro efo/gyda'r car?
     Faint o funiau sbwriel darodd Mr Bean efo/gyda'r car?
2.   *Beth mae o/e'n wisgo gyntaf?*
     Beth wnaeth o/e wisgo gyntaf? etc.
3.   *Sut mae e/o'n gwisgo ei drowsus?*
4.   *Sut mae e/o'n gyrru'r car pan mae e/o'n gwisgo'i drowsus?*
5.   *Sawl gwaith mae'r car yn mynd o gwmpas yr ynys?*
6.   *Pa law mae Mr. Bean yn ei defnyddio i lanhau ei ddannedd?*

For Levels 4/5 and higher

(i)   Watch the first part of the film – until Mr. Bean reaches the car. After viewing, and on the basis of a group discussion, place the following statements in the appropriate order. Not every listed statement is relevant to the clip.

> *Rhoi'r cloc ar y lein i sychu*
> *Mynd allan o'r ystafell*
> *Tynnu'r dillad gwely dros y Tedi*
> *Codi o'r gwely*
> *Deffro*
> *Rhoi'r cloc larwm yn y gwydraid o ddŵr*
> *Mynd i'r tŷ bach*
> *Gwisgo amdano*
> *Agor y cwpwrdd dillad*
> *Clywed y cloc larwm yn canu*
> *Tynnu blewyn o'i drwyn*
> *Tywallt /arllwys 'paned o de*
> *Rhedeg allan i'r car*
> *Rhoi bawd ei droed yn y beipen*
> *Dod yn ôl i'r ystafell*
> *Pigo ei drwyn*
> *Siafio*
> *Cerdded i mewn i'r wal*
> *Gwneud ychydig o ymarfer corff*
> *Gwisgo*
> *Gweld y llun ar yr hongiwr dillad*
> *Llosgi ei droed*

(ii)   Compare your group's version with those of other groups.

(iii)   Watch the clip again to see if you were correct.

Level 6 and higher

(i)   Form groups.

(ii)   Based on discussion, decide on a **group response** to the above statements.

(iii)   Choose a member of the group to report back.

(iv)   Compare your group's responses with those of other groups.

(v)   Re-view the clip.

(vi)   Formulate questions similar to the examples given above.

(vii)   Exchange your group's questions for those of another group.

(viii)   Respond orally to the newly-acquired questions.

The following are examples of books deemed to be suitable for KS1. They contain language that should be familiar to the pupils. They do not necessarily correspond to a particular theme.

Ble maer bêl?	*Cyfres Magi Ann*	*Llyfr 6*
Twm Tân	*Cyfres Magi Ann*	*Llyfr 9*
Y Pry Bach	*Cyfres Magi Ann*	*Llyfr 10*
Parsel i Bawb	*Cyfres Magi Ann*	*Llyfr 11*
Yn y Garej	*Paent Gwlyb*	
Yn y Dŵr	*Paent Gwlyb*	
Ust	*Paent Gwlyb*	
Yr Athrawes	*Paent Gwlyb*	
Peintio'r Drws	*Anifeiliaid Difyr*	
Nadolig Cyntaf Dilys	*Anifeiliaid Difyr*	
Y Cawr Mawr	*Paent Gwlyb*	
Paid	*Paent Gwlyb*	
Teulu Tomos	*Paent Gwlyb*	
Teisen	*Paent Gwlyb*	
Y Sŵ	*Paent Gwlyb*	
Gwyliau	*Paent Gwlyb*	
Ci Clyfar	*Paent Gwlyb*	
Aw!	*Paent Gwlyb*	
Annibendod!	*Paent Gwlyb*	
Y Pengwin	*Paent Gwlyb*	
Yr Arth	*Llyfrau Mawr*	
Gwisgo Babi	*Llyfrau Heulwen*	
Dan Dŵr	*Llyfrau 3D*	
Ble mae Mam Siw?	*Anifeiliaid Difyr*	
Nadolig Cyntaf Siw	*Anifeiliaid Difyr*	
Pen-blwydd Hapus Morgan	*Cyfres Morgan y Morwr (Acen)*	*Stori 1*
Sut mae'r Tywydd?	*Morgan y Morwr*	*Stori 2*
Pacio Bagiau	*Morgan y Morwr*	*Stori 3*
Mynd ar Daith	*Morgan y Morwr*	*Stori 4*

The fact that 'Big Books' can be created out of ordinary-sized books should be constantly borne in mind.

Hwb Cam a Naid	*Pecynnau: Teganau; Dillad; Anifeiliaid; Pobl sy'n Helpu; Bwyd*	
Pen-blwydd Dilys *Pen-blwydd Hapus* *Y Parti*	*Anifeiliaid Difyr* *Paent Gwlyb* *Cyfres Magi Ann*	*Llyfr 3*
Sioe Ffasiwn Siw *Gwisg Ysgol* *Gwisgo* *Coban Doli*	*Anifeiliaid Difyr* *Pecyn 'Dillad'* *Dewi Dinosor* *Cyfres Magi Ann*	*Llyfr 12*
Pero *Smotiau Buwch Goch Gota* *Bili Broga* *Siw a'i Ffrindiau* *Y Tywydd* *Wedi Blino* *Y Pengwin*	*Cyfres Magi Ann* *Pecyn 'Anifeiliaid'* *Llyfrau 3D + tâp* *Anifeiliaid Difyr* *Pecyn 'Anifeiliaid'* *Dewi Dinosor* *Paent Gwlyb*	*Llyfr 8*
Pobl sy'n Helpu *Clinc, Clanc, Clonc* *Helpwch fi!*	*Pecyn 'Pobl sy'n Helpu'* *Cyfres Cil y Drws + Fideo* *Llyfrau 3D + tâp*	
Yn y Caffi *Bwyta Selsig* *Yn y Siop* *Beth wyt ti eisiau?* *Amser Bwyd* *Y Parti* *Cyfres Ddarllen Rhydychen*	*Pecyn 'Bwyd'* *Cyfres Magi Ann* *Anifeiliaid Difyr* *Llyfrau Heulwen* *Morgan y Morwr* *Cyfres Magi Ann* *Drake*	*Llyfr 4* *Stori 5* *Llyfr 3*

LLYFRAU A FIDEOS : ENGHREIFFTIAU O DDEUNYDD ADDAS ar gyfer CA2
BOOKS and VIDEOS : EXAMPLES of MATERIAL SUITABLE for KS 2

YEARS 3 and 4

Taid a'r Sosej	**Llyfrau 3D**
Faint o'r Gloch Draciwla?	**Gwasg Gomer**
Aros Funud	**Cil y Drws + Fideo**
Bwci Bo!	**Anifeiliaid Difyr**
Ble mae Mam Siw?	**Anifeiliaid Difyr**
Lola'r Lindys Barus	**Llyfrau 3D**
Beth ydw i?	**Llyfrau Heulwen**
Beth wyt ti eisiau?	**Llyfrau Heulwen**
Mewn Hen Dŷ	**Llyfrau 3D**
Weithiau	**Cil y Drws + Fideo**
Un Noson Dywyll Dywyll	**Llyfrau 3D**
Diwrnod Braf	**Agor y Drws + Fideo**
Y Meddyg	**Anifeiliaid Difyr**
Snichod	**Story Chest**
Edi Esgus	**Athrawon Bro Clwyd**
Sosej i Carlo	**CBAC/ACCAC + tapiau**
Ticiti Toc	**Gomer/CBAC**
Rholsen Ffigys	**Project Llyfrau Longman**
Cyfres Straeon Sionc	**Gomer**
Cyfres Sbeic ac Eraill	**CBAC**
Iaith Iau 2	**Fideo ail iaith**

YEARS 5 and 6
THEMA BWYD

Y Lindysyn Llwglyd Iawn	**Cyfieithiad o 'The Hungry Caterpillar'**
Lola'r Lindys Barus	**Llyfrau 3D**
Wncwl Em o America	**Cynllun y Canllaw**
Ogla Da (Barddoniaeth)	**CBAC**

Y SYNHWYRAU

Y Dyn Eira	**CBAC**
Bwgan	**Agor y Drws + Fideo**
Trish Trwyn	**Straeon Sionc**

Y TEULU

Dim Problem Sarjant	**Bobol Bach**
Achub y Dydd	**Bobol Bach**
Treinars Newydd Jason	**Bobol Bach**
Dad yn Nofio	**Straeon Sionc**

CHWARAEON

Y Ras *Bydd yn Ofalus Ceri Ann*	*Straeon Sionc* *Agor y Drws + Fideo*

DATHLIADAU

Dwynwen *Weithiau*	*Acen + tâp* *Agor y Drws + Fideo*

GWYLIAU

Gwyliau George *Dewis Gwyliau*	*Fideo* *Agor y Drws + tâp*

COFNODI DARLLEN / READING : KEEPING RECORDS

Mae'n bwysig cadw cofnod o'r hyn sy'n cael ei ddarllen.

A record of books read should be kept.

Yn dilyn mae enghreifftiau o wahanol ffyrdd o gadw cofnod, o'r ddau Gyfnod Allweddol.

There follow examples of different ways of keeping records from both Key Stages.

Enw'r llyfr: ....

Wyt ti'n hoffi'r llyfr?   Ydw [   ]   Nac ydw [   ]

Pam? Dewiswch –

Achos mae o/e'n

dda	ddoniol
ddiflas	drist

Achos mae o/e'n

Ysgrifennwch:
Achos ....

| Beth wyt ti'n hoffi yn y llyfr? |
| Beth dwyt ti ddim yn hoffi yn y llyfr? |

Ysgrifennwch: ....

....

....

....

Tynnwch lun

Enw: --

Dyddiad: --

Enw'r Llyfr --

Enw'r Awdur (*Author*) --

Wyt ti'n hoffi'r llyfr?

Ydw

Nac ydw

Ydw

Nac ydw

Tynnwch lun ac ysgrifennwch:

Enw: --   Dyddiad: ------------------------------

Oed: --

Enw'r Llyfr: ---

Enw'r Awdur: --

Beth oeddet ti'n feddwl o'r llyfr?

Roedd e/o'n --

dda	ddoniol	ofnadwy	gyffrous
wych	drist	ddiflas	ddiddorol★

Ysgrifennwch ---

Tynnwch lun	Geiriau newydd	
	Cymraeg	Saesneg

★(If in doubt about their meanings use the dictionary)

Enw: .... Dyddiad: ....

Oed: ....

Enw'r Llyfr: ....

Enw'r Awdur: ....

Beth oeddet ti'n feddwl o'r llyfr?

Roedd e/o'n ....

dda	ddoniol	ofnadwy	wych	drist
rhy hawdd	gyffrous	ddiflas	ddiddorol	

Cymeriadau/ *Characters*
   Roeddwn i'n hoffi ... / Doeddwn i ddim yn hoffi ...
   achos roedd e/o/hi'n ...
   achos doedd e/o/hi ddim yn ...

Ysgrifennwch am y stori --------------------------------------

----

Tynnwch lun	Geiriau newydd	
	Cymraeg	**Saesneg**

UN FFORDD O YMDRÎN Â STORI

- Darllen stori nes bod y plant yn ei gwybod. (Dylid dewis un sydd yn cynnwys ailadrodd e.e. 'Mewn hen, hen dŷ', neu 'Snichod')
- Canu cân yn seiliedig arni
- Actio'r stori – gan apelio at yr emosiwn a'r dychymyg
- Holi ac Ateb: *Beth arall maen nhw'n fwyta?* etc.

> **Mae Snichod yn bwyta:**
> **hen afal drwg, drwg**
> **hen oren llwyd, llwyd**
> **hen fara o'r bin, etc**
> **A dyna'r gwir i chi.**

- Cael 'Cawod eira' gan gofnodi'r ymateb ar y bwrdd du
- Drilio'r plant mewn cân
- Creu lluniau ar gyfer Llyfr Grŵp
- Rhoi'r llyfr yn y llyfrgell ddosbarth

ONE WAY OF USING A STORY

- Read a story until the children know it. (A story containing much repetition should be chosen e.g. *Mewn hen, hen dŷ* or *Snichod*)
- Sing a song based on the story
- Act out the story appealing to the emotions and the imagination
- Conduct a Question and Answer session: (What else do they eat? etc.) and a brainstorming session recording the feedback on the blackboard

> **Mae Snichod yn bwyta:**
> **hen afal drwg, drwg**
> **hen oren llwyd, llwyd**
> **hen fara o'r bin, etc**
> **A dyna'r gwir i chi.**

- Drill the pupils in song
- Create pictures for a Group Book
- The book can then be filed in the classroom library.

See: 'The Developmental Steps of the Writing Process' in the Methodology section (page 69)			LEVEL
1.	Labelling clothes	– Word and picture association	1
2.	Creating a portrait	– An opportunity to copy and re-combine what has been learnt: • Labelling • Conveying simple information	1 2
3.	Independent copying	– *Ble mae Magi Ann?*	1
4.	Supportive framework 1	– for expressing simple opinions	1
5.	Some reproduction	– *Eisteddfod Llangollen 1*	2
6.	Reconstituting: *Eira*	– short sentences, slight variation of patterns, use of familiar vocabulary. Punctuation and Past Tense used correctly	Level 2 with elements of level 3
7.	More reproduction	– *Eisteddfod Llangollen 2*	2 working towards 3
8.	Supportive framework 2	– *Pentref yr Hendre*	3
9.	Self portrait	– Scott	3
10.	*Tywydd Braf*	–	3 working towards 4
11.	Another supportive framework: *Morris*	– story changed and adapted e.g. the location of *Pryderi y Pry Cop* changed from the sink to the platform and the story adapted to the new location.	4 although the pupil has used the story framework extensively
12.	*Pêl-rwyd* /Netball		5
13.	An example of an adult's written work at **Level 6** of the National Curriculum and **Grade C** *Defnyddio'r Gymraeg* together with the teacher's assessment		6

In the following task, the pupils will introduce themselves within the 'Personal Information' Study Programme. They will work at Level 3. The chart indicates how teachers might prepare pupils for the task as well as the FRAMEWORK that could be used to support them throughout the activity.

Following the framework are comments which a teacher might use in his/her response to the work together with suggestions on ways to improve the standard of the work.

(Adapted from WJEC Second Language INSET material, Ed. Richard Roberts)

AIM OF LEARNING: Expressing a personal opinion about school

STUDY PROGRAMME: Personal Information

HELP FOR THE WRITER
- Introduce/Revise language items such as:
  - *Rydw/Dw/Rwy i'n mynd i …*
  - *Dw i'n/Rwy i'n hoffi + school subjects*
  - *Dw i ddim yn hoffi …*
  - Days of the week
- Pair work: pupils to tell each other which subjects they like/dislike

COMMENTS ON PUPIL'S WORK
- Writes short basic sentences
- Uses suitable and familiar vocabulary and patterns
- The majority of words spelt correctly
- Punctuates using capital letters, commas and full stops

RAISING THE STANDARD OF THE WORK
Pupils should be encouraged to:
- Vary language patterns to a greater degree
- Write consecutive sentences to reflect a grasp of order and sequence

fest

siwmper

menig

côt

cap ✓

crys

sanau

tei

Medi 16

Olivia . Ysgol parc y Llan

Nicole 6 and 3 14

Dyma Nicole

Llygaid brown

gwallt brown

wyneb hapus

Weithiau'n drist

Fy ffrind

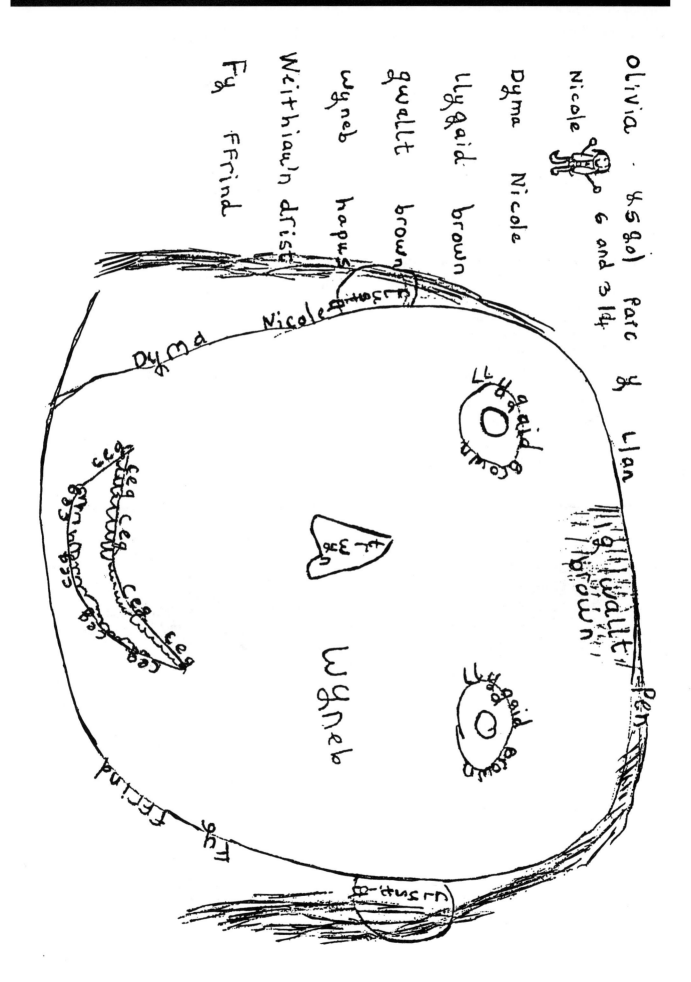

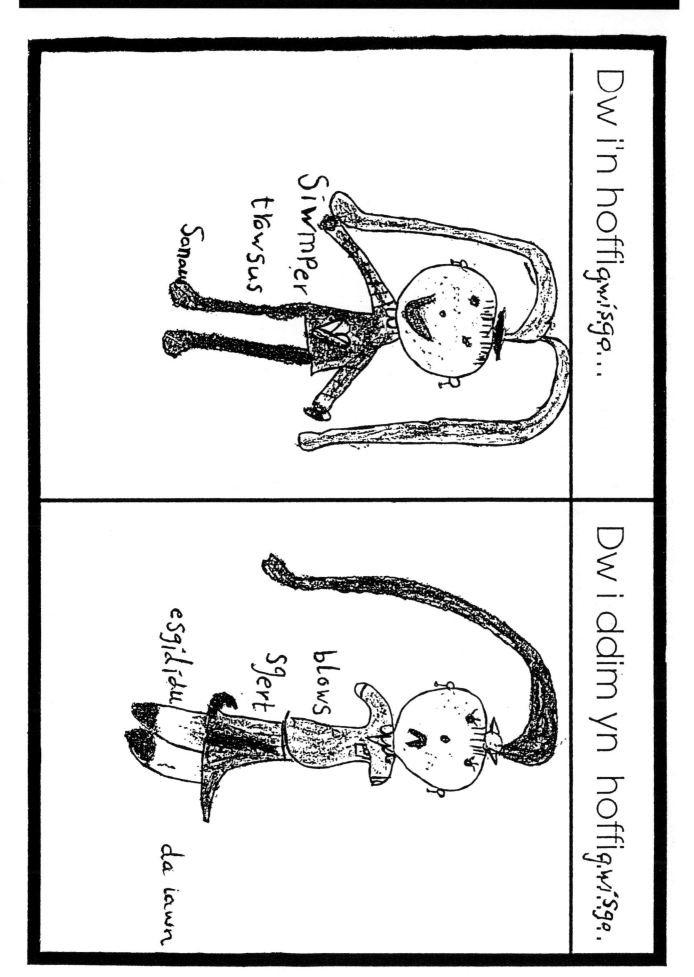

Dw i'n hoffi gwisgo...

Siwmper
tlowsus
sanau

Dw i ddim yn hoffi gwisgo...

blows
sgert
esgidiau

da iawn

Dyma EisteDDFod Llangollen
DwI in hoffi EisteDDDFod
Llangollen.
DwI in hapus ac bendigedig
Mae hyin heulog ac yn
Sych.

ardderchog

*

eira

Roedd hi'n bwrw eira ddoe.
Roeddwn i'n hapus
Mae hi'n bwrw glaw heddiw Do'n hapus hefyd!

By Nia Kennett – orpcror

Dw i'n byw mewn pentref bach o'r enw Hendre.

Mae Hendre yn ymyl tref Yr Wyddgrug.

Mae Yr Wyddgrug yn Sir y Fflint.

Mae Sir y Fflint yng Nghymru.

Dw i'n siarad Cymraeg yn Hendre.

Yn Hendre mae'r tywydd yn ofnadwy.

Mae'n bwrw glaw bob dydd.

Scott ydwi
Dw i'n ddeg oed. Dw i'n byw 9 Bryn Clywedog. Fy hoff raglen teledu Neigbours dw i'n hoffi pêl droed a tenis. dw i ddim yn hoffi pêl rwyd. Fy hoff grwp pop ydy Dire Straits a Bon jovi a Queen. Dw i'n hoffi sglodion a pysgoden a ffa. Dw i'n casau bresych a moron. Dw i'n hoffi lerpwl. Dw i'n hoffi jîns a crys-T a crys a dapiau. Dw i'n hoffi llyfant a reiob a cath. Ar Dydd Sadwrn ydy reidio beic. Dw i'n hoffi i freciost tost a jam a wyau a sosej a ffa. Dw i'n hoffi grovio a brecdanau. Dw i'n hoffe te a patatws a pizza. Dw i'n hoffi super brsgedi a creision a te. Dw i eisiau ar dy benblwydd a pêl droed a dillad. Dw i'n hoffi chwarae marbles a chwarae hoci!

TYWDD BRAF

Dwi'n hoffi chwarae pêl fasged efo
James, Simon, Liam a Martin ar dydd
A Sadwrn ar ôl cinio achos dwi'n hoffi
pêl fasged.

Dwi hoffi hwylio yn y
"optimists" ar y môr yn Bae Golwyn
clwb hwylio efo John Newland ar
dydd Mercher am chwech or 'gloch.

Lefel 4	Level 4
Tystiolaeth o'r canlynol:	Evidence of:
• undod	• cohesion
• brawddegau estynedig	• extended sentences
• amrywio brawddegau	• sentence variation
• prinder gwallau	• few mistakes

Dyma Morris moch bach ydy o.

Mae o'n byw yn platfform yr Gorsaf Reilffo
-rdd.

Dydd Sul. Mae Morris eisiau bwyd ond does dim bwyd.

Dydd Llun. Mae Morris eisian bwyd. Mae cacen odan maink.

Dydd Mawrth. Mae Morris eisian bwyd. Does dim cacen odan maine ond mae cig wrth. bagiau.

O bitti mae Morris yn mynd yn denau

Dydd Mercher. Mae Morris eisiau bwyd eto. Does dim cig wrth bagiau ond mae jeli wrth y ffens. O diar mae Morris yn mynd yn byw.

Dydd Iau. Mae Morris eisiau bwyd. Does dim jeli wrth y ffens ond mae bananas odan y signalau.

bilti mae Morris yn mynd yn fyw ac yn fyw.

Dydd Gwener. Mae Morris eisiau bwyd Dim bananas dan signaliau ond mae pysgod odan ir peiriant tocynnau.

bilti mae Morris yn mynd yn fyw ac yn fyw ac yn fyw ac yn fyw. yn byw ac yn

Dydd Sadwrn. ydy Morris eisiau bwyd?

NAG YDY!

Da iawn.

Dydd Iau   Danielle Gilsenan.   Mawrth 17.
Pelrwyd.
Danielle ydw i. Dwin hoffi pêlrwyd.
Ddaru ni chwarae yn y
tim pelrwyd at Dydd Merchar.
Ddaru ni chwarae etbyn Bod Alaw
Ddaru ni chwarae bendigedig.
Ddaru ni ennill naw-un (9-1).
                                    Tim
pelrwyd yw, Emma, Sarah, Carmela,
Vicky, Katie, Natasha, Kirsty,
Lisa, a fi
            Dwin hoffi chwarae
pelrwyd achos dwin cael hwyl a
maehis ardderchog pan rydyarin
ennill. Rydyn ni
Ddaru ni mynd i chwarae
twrniement mawr yn Bae Colwyn
wythnos nesau ar Mawrth 24.
                                    Baswn
i ennill yr holl twrniement a
cael cwpan.

Lefel 5

- amrywio amser y ferf – presennol; gorffennol; gorberffaith; amodol - baswn
- amrywio person – 1af, 2il, 3ydd unigol 1af lluosog
- achos – rhoi rheswm pam
- dilyniant
- heb fod yn fyr

Level 5

- varies tenses – present; past; pluperfect; conditional – *baswn*
- varies personal forms – 1, 2, 3 singular, 1 plural
- gives reasons to support opinions
- sequential
- not short

1999 Examination Paper

Mary MacGuiness's answers to questions 4 and 5 on the written paper

Q.4 Disgrifiwch lle cawsoch eich magu (50 words):

Mi ges fy magu y Nulyn, yn Iwerddon. Mi wnaeth fy teulu symud o Waterford pan on i chwech wythnos oed. Mi wnaethon ni byw mewn ty yn gogledd y Ddinas. Mi es i i'r ysgol ar cefn beic a Chwareais i efo fy ffrindiau yn y gerddi botaneg. Mi gaethon ni llawer o swn achos roeddwn i'n byw tri milltir o maes awyr dulyn.

Q.5 Sut mae'r ardal lle rydych chi'n byw rwan/nawr yn wahanol? (50 words):

dw i'n byw ym Mangor efo fy teulu rwan. Mae Bangor yn Dinas bach ar ôl Dulyn ond dw i'n ffindio bod bangor yn cyfleus. Mae'n bosib cerdded o gwmpas y ddinas mewn deuddeg munud a mae gynnon ni sinema, siopau, theatr, tai bwyta a tafarnau wrth ochr. Does gynnon ni llawer o draffig trwm fel dulyn.

EXAMINER'S ASSESSMENT

Mary has an oral style. She has a good grasp of the different persons, of the past tense of the verb, the possessive *gan* construction and its corresponding negative form. She can also use clauses introduced by *pan*, *bod* and *achos*. She has correctly used the nasal mutation with Dulyn and Bangor but has omitted several soft mutations. There is evidence of 'selecting suitable vocabulary and phrases' such as *Dulyn, gerddi botaneg, ar cefn beic, efo fy ffrindiau, swn maes awyr Dulyn, deuddeg munud, traffig trwm*. The content of the two questions **appropriately answer the requirements at Level 6** although a candidate at this level could have been expected to display greater mastery of small/capital letters.

To reach Level 7, the mutations should be correct, even in 50 word answers like these.
A firmer grasp of syntax and a more purposeful and assured choice of vocabulary/phrases would also be expected.

- Role-play is a flexible technique and can be used to promote language development at any level.
- It usually reflects what has been taught to and practised by the pupils.
- Various 'stimuli' can be used to initiate the activity, for example: picture-strips, classroom corners which correspond to stories (e.g. a theatre with masks and puppets, a shop, hospital, etc.)
- A written script is another productive stimulus.
- Examples of role-play can be seen in the following section. They exemplify:

A	The kind of considerations language teachers have in mind when creating a script
B	Ways of developing and extending language acquisition at levels 1/2
C	Ways of developing and extending language use at level 2
D(CH)★	The kinds of tasks that can be based on role-play
E(D)	Ways of ensuring that the role-play contains 'information gaps'
F/G(DD/E)	Support for role-play or dialogue using picture strips.

★ The Welsh denotations appear in brackets.

CHWARAE RÔL - YSTYRIAETHAU ATHRAWON WRTH LUNIO SGRIPT
ROLE-PLAY – THE KIND OF CONSIDERATIONS TEACHERS HAVE IN MIND WHEN CREATING A SCRIPT (Level 2)

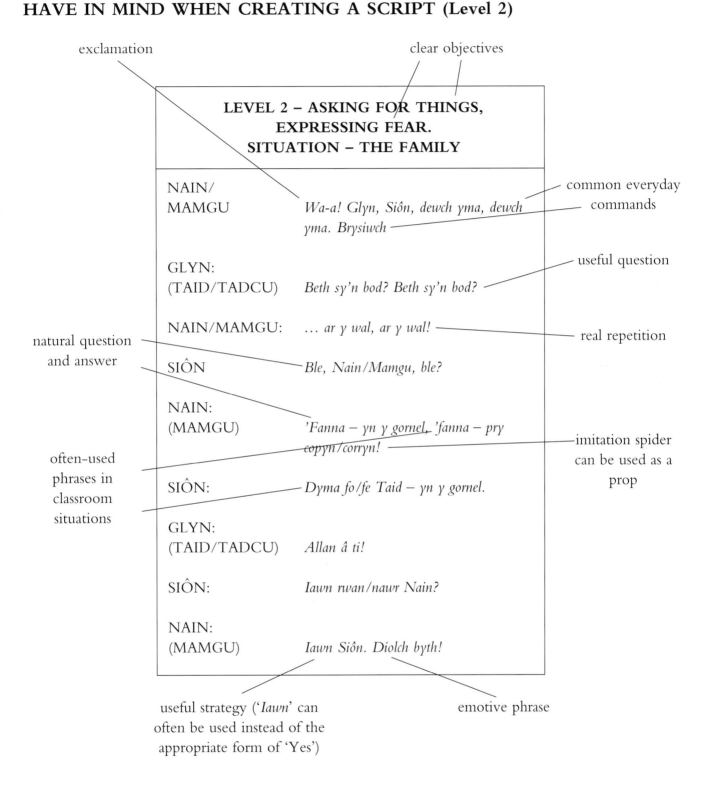

exclamation

clear objectives

LEVEL 2 – ASKING FOR THINGS, EXPRESSING FEAR.
SITUATION – THE FAMILY

NAIN/ MAMGU	*Wa-a! Glyn, Siôn, dewch yma, dewch yma. Brysiwch*
GLYN: (TAID/TADCU)	*Beth sy'n bod? Beth sy'n bod?*
NAIN/MAMGU:	*… ar y wal, ar y wal!*
SIÔN	*Ble, Nain/Mamgu, ble?*
NAIN: (MAMGU)	*'Fanna – yn y gornel, 'fanna – pry copyn/corryn!*
SIÔN:	*Dyma fo/fe Taid – yn y gornel.*
GLYN: (TAID/TADCU)	*Allan â ti!*
SIÔN:	*Iawn rwan/nawr Nain?*
NAIN: (MAMGU)	*Iawn Siôn. Diolch byth!*

common everyday commands

useful question

real repetition

natural question and answer

imitation spider can be used as a prop

often-used phrases in classroom situations

useful strategy ('*Iawn*' can often be used instead of the appropriate form of 'Yes')

emotive phrase

After learning the dialogue, groups of children could work together to **create a new dialogue** by changing some of the elements.

CHWARAE RÔL - DATBLYGU IAITH
ROLE-PLAY – ENCOURAGING LANGUAGE DEVELOPMENT
(Level 1/2)

REINFORCING FAMILIAR LANGUAGE

Hwyl! Bobol Bach!
Mae'n glawio / bwrw glaw — EVERYDAY
Mae'n wyntog — LANGUAGE

REVISION:	POSSIBILITIES:
Ble mae'r ...?	Objects in the class,
ar y ...	pictures from a
yn y ...	familiar story, flash cards.

LEVEL 1/2 – SAYING GOODBYE TALKING ABOUT THE WEATHER. SITUATION – IN THE HOUSE

TOM:	*Hwyl, Mam.*
MAM:	*Hwyl, Tom.*
MAM: (yn edrych drwy'r ffenest)	*O bobol bach! Mae'n glawio / bwrw glaw ac mae'n wyntog.*
TOM:	*Ble mae'r welingtons?*
MAM:	*... wrth y drws.*
TOM:	*O, Mam, mae twll yn y welington!*

EXTENSION
IMITATION
Mae'n glawio / bwrw glaw ac mae'n wyntog
Mae'n glawio / bwrw glaw ac mae'n oer
Mae'n heulog ac mae'n wyntog
Mae'n gymylog ac mae'n oer

PAIR WORK
A. *Mae'n heulog*	SUPPORT with
B. *Ac mae'n wyntog*	weather chart or
A. *Mae'n oer*	flash cards.
B. *Ac mae'n bwrw eira*	

A NEW WORD
- *twll*	Familiar words
Mae twll	*yn y bocs!*
	yn y siwmper!
SUBSTITUTION	*yn y ffenest!*
	yn y tei!

INTRODUCING NEW LANGUAGE

POSSIBILITIES	IMITATION	
Interesting object	*Mae ____ wrth y*	*bwrdd*
		gadair
Children move around the class		*drws*
		bin.
	Mae Bili Broga wrth y	*goeden*
Flash cards		*llyn*
		blodau
Change of vocabulary		

CHWARAE RÔL – DATBLYGU IAITH
ROLE-PLAY – ENCOURAGING LANGUAGE DEVELOPMENT
(Level 2)

REINFORCING FAMILIAR LANGUAGE

Diolch	EVERYDAY
Os gwelwch yn dda	LANGUAGE
Ga i ...... ? Cei.	
Dyna ti	
Ble mae'r ... ?	ESTABLISHED
Yn y ...	LANGUAGE
Dw i ...	

REVISION

1. *... tu ôl i*
POSSIBILITIES
- make a train with the children
  Mae Emma tu ôl i Dylan.
  Mae Dewi tu ôl i Emma.

Sing a SONG (using the above) to the tune "The Farmer wants a wife"

Play a "hunt the object" game and/or a "hunt the child" game

2. *Ga i [siwmper] ? Cei, dyma ti.*
Group work – board games – using small cards with pictures / familiar vocabulary e.g.
CLOTHES   ANIMALS   TOYS

LEVEL 2 – ASKING FOR THINGS, PERSUADING, PROTESTING.
SITUATION – SETTING OUT FOR SCHOOL

A:	*Mam, ble mae'r <u>sudd oren</u>?*
B:	*... yn y bag ysgol*
A:	*Mam, ble mae'r <u>llyfr Cymraeg</u>?*
B:	*... yn y bag ysgol.*
A:	*Mam, ble mae'r <u>bag ysgol</u>?*
B:	*Tu ôl i'r drws.*
A:	*Diolch, Mam. <u>Dych chi'n wych</u>.*
	Ga i siocled os gwelwch yn dda?
A:	*Cei, dyna ti. Ga i sws?*
B:	*O, Mam – dw i'n HWYR!*

EXTENSION

Ble mae'r	*sudd oren?*	*ar y*
	bocs creision?	*yn y*
	bwrdd natur?	*wrth y*
	llyfr Cymraeg?	*dan y*
	siart Cymraeg?	*tu ôl i'r*
	gornel Gymraeg?	*o flaen y*
	bag coch?	
	bag glas?	

INTRODUCING NEW LANGUAGE

Dych chi'n	*wych*	FLASH CARDS
	hwyr	
Dw i'n	*hapus*	MIME
	drist	FACIAL
Rwyt ti'n	*gas*	EXPRESSIONS
familiar language	*swil*	POINTING

TASGAU WEDI EU SEILIO AR CHWARAE RÔL
TASKS THAT CAN BE BASED ON ROLE-PLAY
(Level 1 elementary)

PREPARATION
- revise the 'Food' vocabulary relevant to a party
  e.g. *jeli, sosej, creision, cacen/teisen, siocled, brechdanau*
- use flash cards of favourite characters e.g. from the **Magi Ann** reading series
  Mae Magi Ann yn hoffi jeli / Mae Dicw yn hoffi creision, etc.
- watch a video clip or read a story about a party
- introduce: *Wyt ti'n hoffi _____? Ydw/Nac ydw* – and ask individuals, using toys.
- sing: e.g. to the tune *Migldi Magldi*: *"Magi, wyt ti'n hoffi jeli? Ydw, ydw, ydw wir."*

LEVEL 1 – EXPRESSING LIKES.
SITUATION – AT THE PARTY

Magi Ann:	*Wyt ti'n hoffi jeli?*
Tedi:	*Iym, iym, ydw.*
Magi Ann:	*Wyt ti'n hoffi sosej?*
Tedi:	*Iym, iym, ydw.*
Magi Ann:	*Wyt ti'n hoffi creision?*
Tedi:	*Iym, iym, ydw.*
Magi Ann:	*Beth sy'n bod, Tedi?*
Tedi:	*O-o, dw i'n sâl!*

PAIR WORK
- practise the above language items (using flash cards to support the activity)
- practise *Beth sy'n bod? O-o dwi'n sâl* with appropriate intonation

ROLE PLAY
- get the children to act out the situation with toys or puppets.

FOLLOW-UP WORK
- invite everyone to create a class booklet: *Yn y parti*
- and draw a graph showing the children's favourite party foods

CHWARAE RÔL gyda 'Bylchau gwybodaeth' syml
ROLE-PLAY with simple 'information gaps'
(Level 2)

LEVEL 2 – EXPRESSING LIKES/DISLIKES.

SITUATION – INTERVIEW

A: *Wyt ti'n hoffi _____?*	POSSIBILITIES
B: *Ydw, weithiau.*	*afal, oren,*
	caws, sglodion,
A: *Wyt ti'n hoffi _____?*	*hufen iâ, siocled,*
B: *Ydw, yn fawr iawn.*	*fferins/da da/losin,*
	tomatos, sosej, ham,
A: *Wyt ti'n hoffi _____?*	*pys, sbageti,*
B: *Nac ydw, dim llawer.*	*creision, cyri*
	(py)sgodyn.
A: *Wyt ti'n hoffi _____?*	
B: *Nac ydw, ych a fi!*	

A: *Wyt ti'n hoffi oren?*
B: _____, _____.

A: *Wyt ti'n hoffi siocled?*
B: _____, _____.

A: *Wyt ti'n hoffi tomatos?*
B: _____, _____.

A: *Wyt ti'n hoffi cyri?*
B: _____, _____.

New Language		
weithiau	–	sometimes
wrth gwrs	–	of course
yn fawr iawn	–	very much
dim llawer	–	not a lot
tipyn bach	–	a little bit
ych a fi!	–	Ugh!

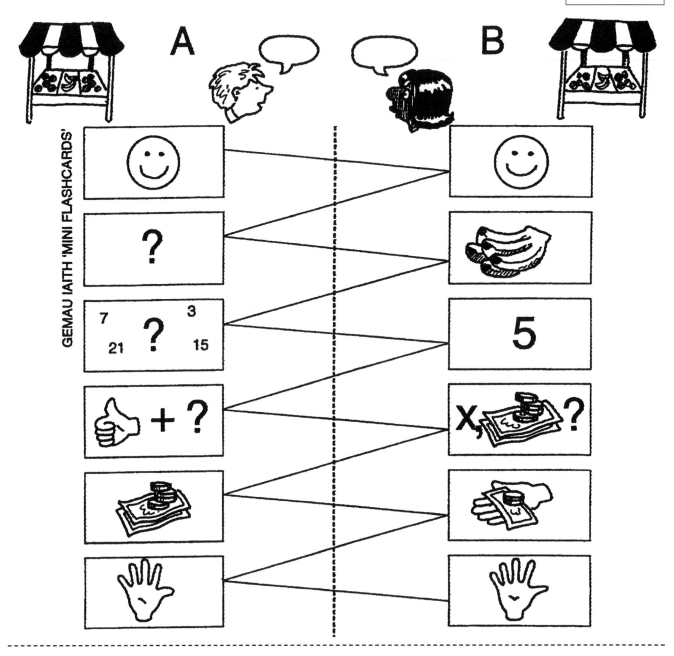

LEVEL/LEFEL 3

Support card to be
used by the pupils
if in difficulty

A	Bore da.
B	Bore da.
A	Ga i helpu?
B	Cewch. Ga i fananas, os gwelwch yn dda?
A	Faint?
B	Pump, os gwelwch yn dda.
A	Dyma chi. Rhywbeth arall?
B	Na, dim byd arall. Faint ydyn nhw?
A	_____ ceiniog, os gwelwch yn dda.
B	Dyma chi.
A	Diolch. Hwyl!
B	Diolch. Hwyl!

CYNNAL CHWARAE RÔL
SUPPORT FOR ROLE-PLAY

A   B

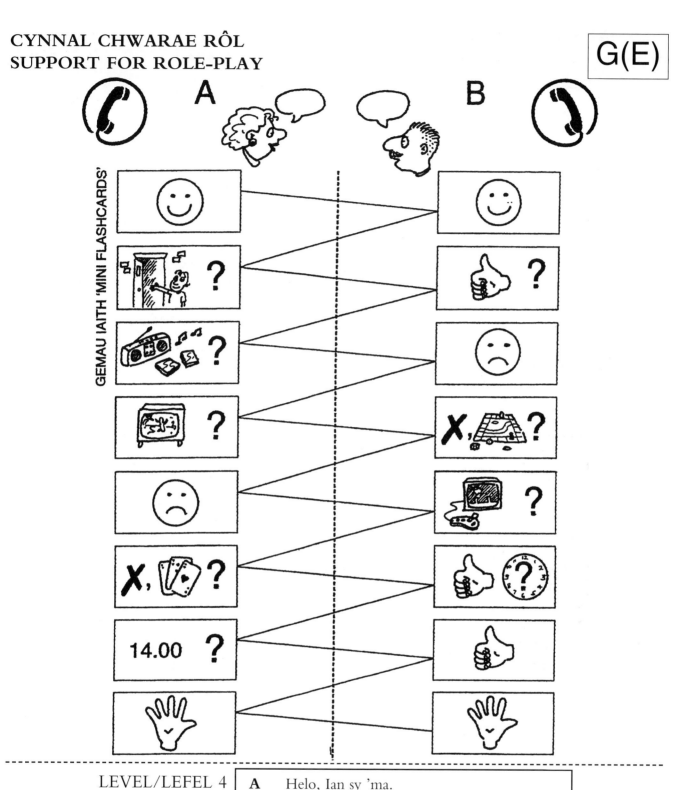

LEVEL/LEFEL 4

Support card to be
used by the pupils
if in difficulty

A	Helo, Ian sy 'ma.
B	Haia?
A	Wyt ti eisiau dod i tŷ ni?
B	Iawn – Beth wnawn ni?
A	Allwn ni wrando ar C.D.
B	Na, dw i ddim yn ffansïo.
A	Gwylio'r teledu?
B	Na, beth am gêm fwrdd?
A	Ych, na, maen nhw'n ddiflas!
B	Gêm gyfrifiadur?
A	Na, beth am gêm o gardiau?
B	Gwych! Wela i di.
A	Hwyl!
B	Hwyl!

GEMAU : ENGHREIFFTIAU O GEMAU DOSBARTH
GAMES: EXAMPLES OF CLASS GAMES

Skills/attributes developed:

- the imagination
- the ability to reason
- the ability to co-operate and socialise
- observation skills

GEMAU ADOLYGU GEIRFA / GAMES FOR VOCABULARY REVISION

1. **RHYTHMS**: LEVEL 1

   Everyone forms a circle on the floor. The teacher begins by clapping his/her hands twice and then clicking the fingers before naming, for example, **a food** such as – *pwdin reis, cyri poeth, jeli coch,* etc.

e.g.	Trainee teacher	–	clap, clap, click,	–	*pwdin reis*
	Child 1	–	clap, clap, click,	–	*siocled brown*
	Child 2	–	clap, clap, click,	–	*sosej tew*

2. **OBJECT GAME** : LEVEL 2

   Everyone forms a **circle**. The teacher chooses an object e.g. a tennis racquet and uses it as anything but a tennis racquet, e.g.

   > *Gwn ydy o. Dw i'n saethu efo gwn.*
   > *Padell ffrïo/ffrimpan ydy o. Dw i'n ffrïo yn y gegin.*

   The object is passed around the circle.
   Every child says an original sentence based on the object.
   If a child is unable to respond the object is passed on to the next child.

3. **WORD TABLE TENNIS**: LEVEL 1

   The teacher chooses a category of words, e.g. parts of the body, colours, countries of Europe.

   Two pupils say words which are related to each other, alternately and without repetition e.g. Pupil 1: *coes*; Pupil 2: *braich*; Pupil 1: *llaw*; Pupil 2: *troed* … When one fails, another pupil comes in to play against the winner. This game can easily be played as a group activity.

   Other possible categories would be: animals, Welsh castles, etc.

4. **CONNECTING WORDS**: LEVEL 1

   Everyone forms a circle. The teacher names a colour e.g. *glas*. Everyone then names objects which have some connection with the colour –
   Pupil 1: *glas*
   Pupil 2: *awyr*
   Pupil 1: *môr*, etc.

5. **CLASSIFYING OBJECTS:** LEVEL 2
    Everyone tries to name objects which have some connection with each other,
    e.g. things found in a house, a school, a toy shop.

6. **CHANTING A RHYME IN A CIRCLE:** LEVEL 2
    e.g. *Mi welais Jac y Do.* The first child says *Mi*, the second *welais*, the third *Jac*, and so on.

7. **THE TEACHER'S CAR:** LEVEL 2/3
    The pupils form a circle or groups. The teacher begins by clapping twice and then clicking the
    fingers as an adjective is added. The clapping and clicking correspond to the following underlined
    words:

Trainee teacher	–	*Mae car yr athrawes yn fach*
Pupil 1	–	*Mae car yr athrawes yn ddu*
Pupil 2	–	*Mae car yr athrawes yn ddel*

    If someone fails, he/she is out of the circle until the next game begins.

    The initial sentence can be widely varied, e.g:

    > *Mae cath yr athrawes yn …*
    > *Mae merch y ffermwr yn …*

GEMAU DISGRIFIO A CHYFARWYDDO / DESCRIBING AND DIRECTING GAMES

1. **THIEF (**Wanted): LEVEL 3/4
    This game can either be played in a circle or as a class. A pupil describes another member of the
    class (without of course looking at that person!). The first one to put a hand on the 'thief's'
    shoulder is the winner. He/She will be the next one to provide a description.

2. **DESCRIBING A SPORTS/TELEVISION PERSONALITY** : LEVEL 3
    The same as 1 but this time if a pupil thinks he/she knows the correct answer, he/she says ' …
    ydych chi' naming a sports/television personality. '*Ga i'ch llofnod* (autograph) *chi?*'

3. **THE ROOM:** LEVEL 1/2
    The teacher asks each pupil to look around the room and observe everything. Then the children
    close their eyes and the teacher asks

e.g	–	*Pa liw ydy'r drws?*
	–	*Sawl ffenest sydd ar agor?*
	–	*Oes llun ar y wal chwith?* etc.

    The children have to respond without opening their eyes.

4. **A VISITOR:** LEVEL 3
The teacher asks a child from another class (or a member of staff) to call in, then asks for a description of him/her when he/she has left.

Games 3 and 4 can be adapted for pair work – Partner A testing Partner B, whose eyes remain closed, before changing roles.

5. **THE SCHOOL**: LEVEL 2
The teacher prepares the children in a previous lesson by asking them to look around the school and observe carefully:

Trainee teacher or individual pupil:
- *Sawl golau sydd yn y neuadd?*
- *Beth ydy lliw carped dosbarth y babanod?* etc

6. **LIKE FINDS LIKE**: LEVEL 2
The pupils are allowed to wander about the hall using a questionnaire asking e.g:
- *Beth ydy maint dy 'sgidiau di*
- *Beth ydy maint dy siwmper di?*
- *Pa liw wyt ti'n hoffi orau?*
- *Pa grŵp pop wyt ti'n hoffi orau?*
- *Beth wyt ti'n hoffi ar y teledu?*

The aim is to find two classmates who have **2** or **3** things in common.

7. **COLOUR**: LEVEL 2
Divide the class into two teams. One team chooses a colour e.g. *coch,* looks for examples of it around the classroom, and makes statements like the following:

- *Mae llyfr <u>o'r lliw yma</u> ar y silff yn y cornel.*
- *Mae sgert <u>o'r lliw yma</u> gan Angela.*
- *Mae paent <u>o'r lliw yma</u> yn y llun ar y wal yn fanna.*

The other team tries to guess the colour.
The task could be adapted for pair work with some pairs eventually reporting back to the rest of the class.

LEVEL: 5   **AIM:** Talk about hobbies

LANGUAGE ITEMS:

Ydych chi?   *Fyddwch chi?*

Wyt ti?   *Fyddi di?*

Pa mor aml … ?

Rwy i / Dw i / mi fydda i / bydda i … unwaith/dwywaith

bob dydd / wythnos / mis/ blwyddyn

bob dydd / bore / pnawn / gyda'r nos

yn ystod y penwythnos / ar nos Sul / ar nos Fercher

yn y bore / prynhawn / yn yr haf / yn y gaeaf

---

ymarfer, beicio, chwarae golff, chwarae tenis, nofio, cerdded, dringo, sgïo, hedfan, gyrru, peintio, arlunio, gwneud crochenwaith, cerflunio, tynnu lluniau, parasiwtio, dawnsio, coginio, gwnïo/pwytho, gwneud gwaith coed, canu'r piano, chwarae'r ffidil, gwrando ar y radio, gwrando ar recordiau, darllen, gwylio'r teledu, ysgrifennu llythyrau, gwneud ioga, gweu, darllen, gwylio, gwneud … , trïo/ceisio … , eisiau …

NUMBER OF PLAYERS – eight or more

RESOURCES
- Cards and questionnaires for each player
- The relevant information on the cards

HOW TO PLAY THE GAME
- Members of the group circulate and ask each other questions e.g:
     Wyt ti/ Ydych chi'n gallu chwarae/canu'r piano?
     Wyt ti /Ydych chi'n gwylio'r teledu?
- They then complete the questionnaire based on answers received.
- At the end of the task they report back to the members of other groups.

The **level of the work** can be changed using different constructions.

The present game is intended for pupils on Level 5. It could be adapted for use at any level.

PA OFFER WYT TI ANGEN?
(What equipment do you need?)

Rwy/Dw i angen tywel a gogls i nofio

Mae'r gweithgaredd hwn yn defnyddio'r un lluniau â 'Ffeindio Partner' (t. 97 a 98)
The activity re-uses the pictures found on pages 97 and 98.

PA OFFER WYT TI EISIAU?
(What equipment do you want?)

Rwy/Dw i eisiau tywel a gogls i nofio

Mae'r gweithgaredd hwn yn defnyddio'r un lluniau â 'Ffeindio Partner' (t. 97 a 98)

The activity re-uses the pictures found on pages 97 and 98.

Ble mae Madrid?	Ble mae Paris?	Ble mae Aberdeen?	Ble mae Birmingham?
Oes eliffant yn y dosbarth?	Oes parot yn y dosbarth?	Oes llyfrgell yn y dref?	Oes twˆr yn Blackpool?
Ydy Pete Sampras yn chwarae tennis?	Ydy David Beckham yn chwarae rygbi?	Ydy Rhyl yn Sbaen?	Ydy Oslo yn Norwy?
Ydych chi'n hoffi nofio?	Ydych chi'n gallu hedfan?	Ydych chi'n gallu reidio beic?	Ydych chi'n byw yn Sbaen?

The present game is intended to enable pupils to revise the question forms – at Level 3. It could however be adapted for use at any level.

RHAGLENNI CYFRIFIADUROL A CHRYNO DDISGIAU DEFNYDDIOL
USEFUL COMPUTER PROGRAMMES AND COMPACT DISCS

Information on useful computer programmes and compact discs can be found in the catalogues of the following agencies:

- MEU Wales
- Welsh Joint Education Committee (WJEC)
- Welsh Books Council
- ACCAC
- Local Education Authorities
- Further Education and Higher Education Institutions
- Canolfan Bedwyr, University of Wales, Bangor.

Useful websites:
- www.learn-ict.org.uk/links/lnx_cymraeg00.asp
- www.drws.co.uk/en/

Part 4
Video Examples of Oral and Reading Work with Explanatory Notes

SAMPLING ORAL STANDARDS

The following statements are not intended to be definitive assessments but are offered in order to stimulate discussion about the content of the clips, based on the standards.

EXAMPLE 1: GROUP 1
The group attains **Level 2**. The nature of the conversation is elementary, with only a **modicum** of variation to be seen in vocabulary and structure.

EXAMPLE 2:
A good **Level 3**, but the group has not yet mastered the variety of phrases and sentence patterns necessary to reach **Level 4**. The ability to ask questions has not developed to the same extent as the ability to respond.

EXAMPLE 3: GROUP 2
Here the conversation is often fluid and the responses extended. They reach **Level 4** with elements of **Level 5** as they ' show more confidence … and offer some simple reasons to explain their ideas'.

EXAMPLE 4: GROUP 3
There is a considerable variety within the group. Two members are on **Levels 2 and 3 but** are able to follow and understand at a higher level. But they do not have the confidence to use a range of sentence structures to ask questions and respond. The two who excel speak 'freely and with reasonable accuracy in a variety of situations and contexts and exhibit a reasonably good grasp of the natural syntax of the spoken language'. They reach **Levels 5, 6** and occasionally display definite elements of **Level 7.**

EXAMPLE 5: GROUP 4
As a whole, the group reaches a secure **Level 6**. However, individuals within the group exhibit definite elements of **Level 7**, e.g. paying 'attention to sequence by developing their conversation deliberately … speaking freely and with reasonable accuracy in different situations and contexts … ', and even **Level 8** e.g. 'speaking freely and accurately on the whole, and exhibiting quite a secure grasp of the natural syntax of the spoken language'.